중등 영어 교재의 베스트셀러

중등 영어 문법 실력 쌓기!

Grammar Builder

5

Grammar Builder 5

ⓒ2015 by I am Books

지은이	이상건
펴낸이	신성현, 오상욱
펴낸곳	도서출판 아이엠북스
	153-802 서울시 금천구 가산디지털2로 14 1116호 (대륭테크노타운 12차)
대표전화	02-6343-0999
팩스	02-6343-0995
출판등록	2006년 6월 7일
	제 313-2006-000122호
ISBN	978-89-6398-101-7 63740

www.iambooks.co.kr

중등 영어 문법 실력 쌓기!

Grammar Builder

You Are the Only One!

5

Introduction Grammar Builder는?

■ 이 책의 성격

문법 개념 설명부터 마무리 확인까지 실용 문제로 구성된 기본 영어 문법서

■ 이 책의 학습 목표 및 특징

- 다양하고 많은 문제를 통해 실전 문법을 익히고 영어 교과 과정을 대비한다.
- 이해하기 쉽게 설명한 문법의 개념과 원리를 바탕으로 문제를 통해 실력을 향상시킨다.
- 핵심 문법 개념을 이해하고 점진적으로 확장된 문제를 통해 문법 원리를 익힌다.
- 문법 학습뿐만 아니라 문장 패턴 학습과 기초 문장 영작을 통해 문장 쓰기를 훈련한다.
- 서술형 비중이 커지는 추세를 반영하여 학업 성취도 및 서술형 평가를 대비한다.

■ 이 책에 대한 세부 사항

- 문법 개념 설명부터 마무리 확인까지 문제 형식으로 구성하여 실전에 강하도록 하였다.
- 선택형 문제, 단답형 쓰기, 문장 패턴 쓰기로 확장하며 실력을 향상하도록 구성하였다.
- 단어와 문장을 정리하여 사전에 학습함으로 자연스럽게 문법 학습이 이루어지도록 하였다.
- 실전 문제와 서술형 문제를 강화하여 문법 개념과 원리를 응용할 수 있도록 하였다.

■ 이 책을 활용한 영어 문법 실력 쌓기

1. 문법 학습 전 정리된 단어와 문장을 먼저 예습한다.
   - 단어와 문장을 알면 어렵게 느껴지는 문법도 쉽게 학습할 수 있다.

2. 문법은 이해+암기이다. 필요한 문법 사항은 암기한다.
   - 문법의 쓰임과 역할을 이해하고 암기하여 필요할 때 적용하는 것이 좋다.

3. 문법을 학습할 때 예문을 통해 문법 개념을 학습한다.
   - 예문을 문법적으로 파악하면 문장이 복잡해도 쉽게 이해할 수 있다.

4. 문제를 푸는 것으로 끝내지 않고 대화나 글로 마무리한다.
   - 문법을 배우는 이유는 글을 이해하고 쓸 수 있는 능력을 갖추기 위한 것이다.

Grammar Series Contents

contents

About This Book 구성 및 특징

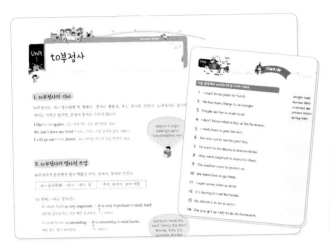

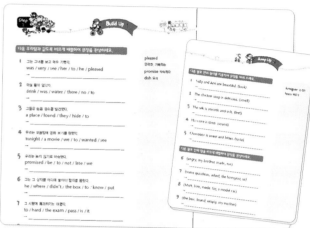

1. Unit별 핵심 문법 개념 정리

Unit별 학습목표를 제시하여 중점 사항을 파악하 도록 하였고, 기초적인 문법 사항을 쉽게 이해할 수 있도록 설명하여 문법 개념 이해를 돕습니다. 또한 다양한 예문을 통해 문법 원리 학습을 적용 하여 이해하도록 하였습니다.

2. Step 1 - Check Up

학습목표와 핵심문법 개념에 대한 기초적인 확인 문제로 구성하여 문법 원리를 문제를 통해서 익히 도록 구성하였습니다. 스스로 풀어보면서 반복 학 습을 통해 문법의 규칙을 이해하도록 하였습니다.

3. Step 2 - Build Up

다양한 형식의 다소 난이도 있는 문제로 구성하여 앞에서 배운 내용을 복습하며 문법 원리를 익히도 록 하였습니다. 학습한 내용을 본격적으로 적용하 고 응용해 보면서 다양한 유형을 연습하도록 하였 습니다.

4. Step 3 - Jump Up

핵심 문법 개념을 스스로 정리해 보도록 하여 이 해도를 확인하고 보완하도록 하였으며 확장형 응 용문제를 통해 학습 목표를 성취하도록 하였습니 다. 또한 영작문 실력이 향상되도록 서술형 문제 위주로 구성하였습니다.

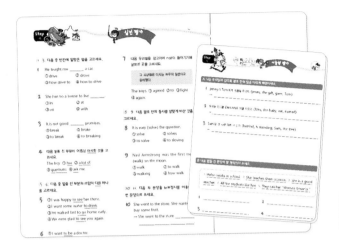

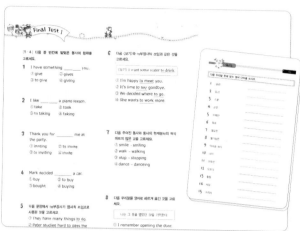

5. Step 4 – 실전 평가

Unit별 핵심 문법 개념과 다양한 문제로 익힌 문법 사항을 마무리 테스트로 구성하여 스스로 점검해 보도록 하였습니다. 이를 통해 문법 문제에 대한 응용력을 키우고 시험 유형에 대비하도록 하였습니다.

6. Step 5 – 서술형 평가

점점 서술형 비중이 커지는 추세를 반영하여 영작문 위주로 구성된 Unit별 종합 문제를 풀어보면서 Unit을 정리하고 학업성취도 평가 및 서술형 평가를 대비하도록 하였습니다.

7. Final Test

본 교재를 통해서 배운 핵심 문법 개념과 문법 사항을 종합평가로 풀어보면서 정리하고 마무리하도록 하였습니다. 종합적으로 배운 내용을 확인하고 점검하도록 하였습니다.

8. Words in Grammar

본 교재의 본문에 사용된 단어들과 문장을 정리하여 문법 학습에 활용하도록 하였습니다. 예습으로 단어를 학습하고 학습 집중도를 올리도록 활용하는 것이 좋습니다.

Curriculum

Book	Month	Week	Hour	Unit	
1	**1**	1	1	1. 문장의 기본 구성	Words 활용
			2		서술형 평가
		2	1	2. 셀 수 있는 명사	Words 활용
			2		서술형 평가
		3	1	3. 셀 수 없는 명사	Words 활용
			2		서술형 평가
		4	1	4. 관사	Words 활용
			2		서술형 평가
	2	1	1	5. 인칭대명사와 격변화	Words 활용
			2		서술형 평가
		2	1	6. 지시대명사, 지시형용사	Words 활용
			2		서술형 평가
		3	1	7. be동사의 현재시제	Words 활용
			2		서술형 평가
		4	1	8. be동사의 부정문, 의문문	Words 활용
			2		서술형 평가
2	**3**	1	1	1. 일반동사의 현재시제	Words 활용
			2		서술형 평가
		2	1	2. 일반동사의 부정문, 의문문	Words 활용
			2		서술형 평가
		3	1	3. There is/are, 비인칭주어 it	Words 활용
			2		서술형 평가
		4	1	4. 형용사	Words 활용
			2		서술형 평가
	4	1	1	5. Some, Any, All, Every	Words 활용
			2		서술형 평가
		2	1	6. 수량형용사	Words 활용
			2		서술형 평가
		3	1	7. 부사	Words 활용
			2		서술형 평가
		4	1	8. 현재진행형	Words 활용
			2		서술형 평가
3	**5**	1	1	1. 기수와 서수	Words 활용
			2		서술형 평가
		2	1	2. 부정대명사, 재귀대명사	Words 활용
			2		서술형 평가
		3	1	3. 비교 구문	Words 활용
			2		서술형 평가
		4	1	4. 조동사	Words 활용
			2		서술형 평가

Grammar Builder 시리즈는 총 5권으로 구성되어 있으며, 권당 8주(2개월) 16차시(Unit당 2차시 수업)로 학습할 수 있도록 구성하였습니다. 주 2회 수업을 기준으로 하였으며 학습자와 학습 시간에 따라 변경이 가능합니다.

Book	Month	Week	Hour	Unit	
3	6	1	1	5. 동사의 과거시제	Words 활용
			2		서술형 평가
		2	1	6. 과거시제의 부정문, 의문문	Words 활용
			2		서술형 평가
		3	1	7. 과거진행형	Words 활용
			2		서술형 평가
		4	1	8. 동사의 미래시제	Words 활용
			2		서술형 평가
4	7	1	1	1. 의문사 의문문	Words 활용
			2		서술형 평가
		2	1	2. 의문대명사와 의문형용사	Words 활용
			2		서술형 평가
		3	1	3. 의문부사	Words 활용
			2		서술형 평가
		4	1	4. 명령문	Words 활용
			2		서술형 평가
	8	1	1	5. 감탄문	Words 활용
			2		서술형 평가
		2	1	6. 접속사	Words 활용
			2		서술형 평가
		3	1	7. 전치사	Words 활용
			2		서술형 평가
		4	1	8. 부정의문문, 부가의문문	Words 활용
			2		서술형 평가
5	9	1	1	1. to부정사	Words 활용
			2		서술형 평가
		2	1	2. 동명사	Words 활용
			2		서술형 평가
		3	1	3. 현재분사와 과거분사	Words 활용
			2		서술형 평가
		4	1	4. 문장의 형식 1	Words 활용
			2		서술형 평가
	10	1	1	5. 문장의 형식 2	Words 활용
			2		서술형 평가
		2	1	6. 현재완료	Words 활용
			2		서술형 평가
		3	1	7. 수동태	Words 활용
			2		서술형 평가
		4	1	8. 관계대명사	Words 활용
			2		서술형 평가

Unit 1

to부정사

to부정사의 명사적 쓰임을 이해하고 활용할 수 있다.

to부정사의 형용사적 쓰임을 이해하고 활용할 수 있다.

to부정사의 부사적 쓰임을 이해하고 활용할 수 있다.

부정사는 '정해지지 않은 말'이라는 뜻으로 그 쓰임이 하나로 정해져 있지 않고 다양하기 때문에 붙여진 이름이에요. 동사가 to부정사가 되면 동사의 의미는 그대로 가지고 있지만, 그 쓰임은 더 이상 동사로 쓰이지 않아요. to부정사는 문장에 따라 명사, 형용사, 부사로 쓰여요.

Unit 1 to부정사

1. to부정사의 의미

to부정사는 'to+동사원형'의 형태로, 명사나 형용사, 또는 부사로 쓰인다. to부정사는 동사의 의미는 가지고 있지만, 문장의 동사로 쓰이지 않는다.

I like to eat apples. 나는 사과 먹는 것을 좋아한다. [명사]
We don't have any food to eat. 우리는 먹을 음식이 없다. [형용사]
I will go out to eat dinner. 나는 저녁을 먹으러 나갈 것이다. [부사]

> 일정하게 그 쓰임이
> 정해져 있지 않아서
> '부정사(不定詞)'라고 한다.

2. to부정사의 명사적 쓰임

to부정사가 문장에서 명사 역할인 주어, 목적어, 보어로 쓰인다.

to+동사원형: ~하기, ~하는 것	주어, 목적어, 보어 역할

(1) 주어: ~하는 것이(은)

To study hard is very important. = It is very important to study hard.
열심히 공부를 하는 것은 매우 중요하다. └─ 가주어 it

To read books is interesting. = It is interesting to read books.
책을 읽는 것은 재미있다. └─ 가주어 it

> to부정사 주어는
> 항상 단수 취급한다.

> to부정사가 주어인 경우,
> 주어가 길어지는 것을 피하기
> 위해 it을 주어로 삼고
> to부정사를 문장 뒤로
> 보낼 수 있다.

(2) 목적어: ~하는 것을, ~하기를

I like to see the movies. 나는 영화 보는 것을 좋아한다.

I don't want to eat pizza now. 나는 피자 먹기를 원하지 않는다. (먹기 싫다.)

He promised not to be late again. 그는 다시는 늦지 않을 것을 약속했다.

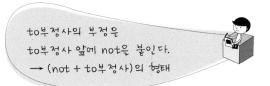

to부정사의 부정은
to부정사 앞에 not을 붙인다.
→ (not + to부정사)의 형태

(3) 보어: ~하는 것이다

My dream is to be a singer. 나의 꿈은 가수가 되는 것이다.

My hobby is to take pictures. 나의 취미는 사진을 찍는 것이다.

Pop Quiz   I. 다음 문장에서 to부정사를 찾아 밑줄을 그으세요.

❶ I like to play soccer.   ❷ To sing a song is fun.

3. to부정사의 형용사적 쓰임

to부정사가 명사 뒤에 와서 형용사 역할을 하며 명사를 수식한다.

to＋동사원형: ~할, ~하는	명사 뒤에서 명사를 수식

I want some water to drink. 나는 마실 물을 원한다.

He needs a cap to put on. 그는 쓸 모자를 필요로 한다.

We have many things to do tonight. 우리는 오늘 밤에 해야 할 일이 많다.

4. to부정사의 부사적 쓰임

to부정사가 부사 역할을 하며 동사나 형용사를 수식한다.

to + 동사원형: ~해서, ~하기 위해서	목적이나 감정의 원인

(1) 목적: ~하려고, ~하기 위해

I study hard **to pass** the exam. 나는 그 시험에 통과하기 위해 열심히 공부한다.

We got up early **to have** breakfast. 우리는 아침을 먹기 위해 일찍 일어났다.

(2) 감정의 원인: ~해서

I am so glad **to hear** the news. 나는 그 소식을 들어서 매우 기쁘다.

She was shocked **to meet** him. 그녀는 그를 만나서 충격을 받았다.

5. 의문사+to부정사의 쓰임

의문사와 to부정사가 결합하여 문장에서 명사처럼 사용되며 '~해야 할지'로 해석한다.

의문사 + to부정사: ~해야 할지	목적어 역할(명사)

I don't know **what to do** next. 나는 다음에 무엇을 해야 할지를 모르겠다.

He knows **where to go**. 그는 어디로 가야 할지를 안다.

She decided **when to leave** here. 그녀는 여기에서 언제 떠날지를 결정했다.

They know **how to go**. 그들은 어떻게 가야 할지를(가는 방법을) 안다.

Pop Quiz

2. 다음 주어진 말을 to부정사로 바꾸어 쓰세요.

❶ I have no money _____ you. (lend)

❷ I went to the store _____ clothes. (buy)

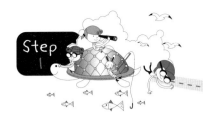 
다음 문장에서 to부정사에 동그라미 하세요.

1 I want to eat pizza for lunch.

2 He has many things to do tonight.

3 People use fire to make food.

4 I don't know what to buy at the bookstore.

5 I study hard to pass the test.

6 She was sad to see the poor boy.

7 He went to the library to borrow books.

8 They were surprised to meet him there.

9 The soldiers came to protect us.

10 We knew how to go there.

11 I want some water to drink.

12 It is boring to read the books.

13 My dream is to be an actor.

14 The boy got up early to do his homework.

15 He wants to learn more about art.

16 To exercise is very good for your health.

tonight 오늘밤
borrow 빌리다
surprised 놀란
protect 보호하다
boring 지루한

다음 문장에서 to부정사가 수식하는 말에 동그라미 하세요.

living 살아 있는
hide 숨다
plan 계획
way 방법, 길
place 장소

1   The people need houses to live in.

2   Please give me a computer to use.

3   They have many books to read.

4   All living things need water to drink.

5   I want a new piano to play.

6   There is a lot of food to eat.

7   We have nothing to give you.

8   They need some cookies to eat.

9   They have a big room to stay.

10   He has something to hide.

11   It is time to say goodbye.

12   Do you have any plan to see a movie?

13   They need some paper to write on.

14   There were many things to do yesterday.

15   Do you know the way to get there?

16   There are many places to visit in Seoul.

다음 주어진 동사를 to부정사로 바꿔 쓰세요.

get 얻다, 받다
novel 소설
solve 풀다
machine 기계

1 She was sorry _____ the news. (hear)

2 The girl went there _____ a pencil. (buy)

3 Sally wants _____ a painter. (is)

4 I am so happy _____ him. (see)

5 It is very boring _____ Japanese. (study)

6 Matt hoped _____ this town. (leave)

7 He was glad _____ a new car. (get)

8 We decided _____ a taxi. (take)

9 Judy was pleased _____ her mother. (meet)

10 We came _____ them. (help)

11 She knows what _____ tomorrow. (do)

12 _____ novels is interesting. (read)

13 My dream is _____ a great scientist. (is)

14 It is important _____ to school. (go)

15 I started _____ the problems. (solve)

16 He doesn't know how _____ the machine. (use)

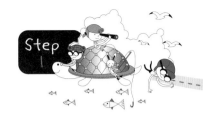

다음 주어진 동사를 이용하여 우리말과 같도록 알맞은 말을 쓰세요.

future 미래
vistor 방문객
wish 소원

1 그때 눈이 오기 시작했다. (snow)

→ It started _____ _____ that time.

2 그는 그의 오랜 친구를 만나서 반가웠다. (meet)

→ He was glad _____ _____ at his old friend.

3 너는 미래에 무엇을 하고 싶니? (do)

→ What would you like _____ _____ in the future?

4 나의 취미는 피아노를 연주하는 것이다. (play)

→ My hobby is _____ _____ the piano.

5 Ann은 꽃들을 사기 위해 가게에 갔다. (buy)

→ Ann went to a shop _____ _____ flowers.

6 CD 플레이어 사용하는 방법을 알려주세요. (use)

→ Please tell me how _____ _____ the CD player.

7 그는 그 방문객들을 보기 위해 역에 갔다. (see)

→ He went to the station _____ _____ the visitors.

8 나의 소원은 선물을 많이 받는 것이다. (get)

→ My wish is _____ _____ many presents.

9 매일 운동하는 것은 매우 어렵다. (exercise)

→ It is very hard _____ _____ every day.

10 나는 이 음식을 만들기 위해 당근이 필요하다. (make)

→ I need carrots _____ _____ this dish.

다음 주어진 동사를 이용하여 우리말과 같도록 알맞은 말을 쓰세요.

coin 동전

grocery 식료품

pleased 기쁜

plant 식물

1 그녀의 취미는 동전을 모으는 것이다. (collect)

→ Her hobby is _____ _____ coins.

2 그들은 약간의 식료품을 사기 위해 거기에 갔다. (buy)

→ They went there _____ _____ some groceries.

3 나는 너에게 줄 것이 아무것도 없다. (give)

→ I have nothing _____ _____ you.

4 사람들이 그의 노래들을 좋아하기 시작했다. (like)

→ People started _____ _____ his songs.

5 많은 아이들이 햄버거 먹는 것을 좋아한다. (eat)

→ Many kids like _____ _____ hamburgers.

6 그것을 들으니 유감이다. (hear)

→ I am sorry _____ _____ that.

7 너는 여행할 계획이 있니? (travel)

→ Do you have any plan _____ _____?

8 그 학생들은 집으로 돌아가기를 원했다. (go)

→ The students wanted _____ _____ back home.

9 우리는 우리의 일을 마쳐 기뻤다. (finish)

→ We were pleased _____ _____ our work.

10 모든 식물들은 살기 위해 물이 필요하다. (live)

→ All the plants need water _____ _____.

다음 우리말과 같도록 알맞은 말을 쓰세요.

dark 어두운

history 역사

happiness 행복

1 모든 사람들은 살 집이 필요하다.

→ All the people need houses _____ _____ in.

2 나는 새 자전거가 생겨서 무척 행복했다.

→ I was so happy _____ _____ a new bicycle.

3 그녀는 어두운 곳에서 자는 것을 싫어한다.

→ She hates _____ _____ in the dark.

4 그는 컴퓨터를 사용하는 법을 배웠다.

→ He learned _____ _____ _____ a computer.

5 John은 역사에 대해 더 많이 공부하고 싶어 한다.

→ John wants _____ _____ more about history.

6 그녀는 여배우가 되고 싶어 한다.

→ She wants _____ _____ an actress.

7 우리는 어디로 가야 할지 결정했다.

→ We decided _____ _____ _____.

8 우리는 점심을 먹을 시간이 없었다.

→ We didn't have time _____ _____ lunch.

9 그녀는 그때 무엇을 해야 할지 몰랐다.

→ She didn't know _____ _____ _____ then.

10 네 가족을 사랑하는 것은 너에게 행복을 준다.

→ _____ _____ your family gives you happiness.

Build Up 1

다음 우리말과 같도록 바르게 배열하여 문장을 완성하세요.

1 그는 그녀를 보고 매우 기뻤다.

was / very / see / her / to / he / pleased

→ _____

2 마실 물이 없었다.

drink / was / water / there / no / to

→ _____

3 그들은 숨을 장소를 발견했다.

a place / found / they / hide / to

→ _____

4 우리는 오늘밤에 영화 보기를 원했다.

tonight / a movie / we / to / wanted / see

→ _____

5 우리는 늦지 않기로 약속했다.

promised / be / to / not / late / we

→ _____

6 그는 그 상자를 어디에 놓아야 할지를 몰랐다.

he / where / didn't / the box / to / know / put

→ _____

7 그 시험에 통과하기는 어렵다.

to / hard / the exam / pass / is / it

→ _____

8 나는 이 요리를 만들기 위해서 양파가 필요하다.

this dish / onions / I / to / make / need

→ _____

pleased
만족한, 기뻐하는

promise 약속하다

dish 요리

다음 우리말과 같도록 바르게 배열하여 문장을 완성하세요.

vet 수의사
same 같은
necessary 필요한

1 나에게 그 기계를 사용하는 방법을 말해 주세요.

tell / please / to / the machine / use / how / me

→ _____

2 나는 너에게 줄 무엇인가 있다.

something / you / to / have / give / I

→ _____

3 나의 꿈은 수의사가 되는 것이다.

dream / be / to / is / my / a vet

→ _____

4 Jack은 운동화를 사기 위해 가게에 갔다.

went / Jack / to / buy / a store / sneakers / to

→ _____

5 같은 것들에 대해 계속 이야기하는 것은 지루하다.

is / to / talk about / it / the same things / boring

→ _____

6 나는 그 자동차를 살 약간의 돈이 있다.

I / some money / to / the car / have / buy

→ _____

7 음악 수업을 듣는 것은 필요하다.

take / necessary / a music lesson / is / it / to

→ _____

8 Dan은 나에게 무엇을 요리해야 할지 물었다.

me / what / Dan / asked / to / cook

→ _____

Build Up 3

rude 무례한
impossible 불가능한
habit 습관

다음 문장과 뜻이 같도록 빈칸에 알맞은 말을 쓰세요.

1 To swim in this river is dangerous.

→ _____ is dangerous _____ _____ in this river.

2 To remember his phone number is difficult.

→ _____ is difficult _____ _____ his phone number.

3 To ask someone's age is rude.

→ _____ is rude _____ _____ someone's age.

4 To understand this poem is impossible.

→ _____ is impossible _____ _____ this poem.

5 To break a bad habit is hard.

→ _____ is hard _____ _____ a bad habit.

다음 괄호 안의 말을 바르게 배열하여 문장을 완성하세요.

6 I don't know (to, where, put) the bag. → _____

7 Tell me (when, open, to) the door. → _____

8 She asked me (use, to, how) it. → _____

9 I didn't decide (what, cook, to). → _____

10 Can you tell me (how, get, to) there? → _____

11 We don't decide (do, to, what). → _____

12 He told me (to, go, where) first. → _____

to부정사 · **25**

다음 빈칸에 알맞은 말을 쓰세요.

1 to부정사는 'to + _____'의 형태로, 명사나 _____, 또는 부사로 쓰인다. to부정사는 동사의 의미는 가지고 있지만, 문장의 _____로 쓰이지 않는다.

2 to부정사의 명사적 쓰임은 to부정사가 문장에서 '~하는 것, ~하기'라는 뜻으로 명사로 쓰여 _____, _____, _____ 역할을 한다.

3 to부정사 주어는 항상 _____ 취급하며, to부정사가 주어일 경우에 _____가 길어지는 것을 피하기 위해 _____을 주어로 쓰고 to부정사를 문장 뒤로 보낼 수 있다.

4 to부정사의 부정은 to부정사 앞에 _____을 붙인다. → _____ + to부정사의 형태

5 to부정사의 형용사적 쓰임은 to부정사가 _____ 뒤에 와서 _____ 역할을 하며 명사를 수식한다.

6 to부정사의 부사적 쓰임은 to부정사가 _____ 역할을 하며 동사나 형용사를 수식한다. '~하기 위해, ~해서'라는 뜻으로 _____이나 감정의 _____을 나타낸다.

7 _____와 to부정사가 결합하여 문장에서 _____처럼 사용되며 '~해야 할지'로 해석한다.

I don't know _____ to do next. 나는 다음에 무엇을 해야 할지를 모르겠다.

He knows _____ to go. 그는 어디로 가야 할지를 안다.

She decided _____ to leave here. 그녀는 여기에서 언제 떠날지를 결정했다.

They know _____ to go. 그들은 어떻게 가야 할지를(가는 방법을) 안다.

다음 문장에서 밑줄 친 부분을 바르게 고쳐 쓰세요.

flour 밀가루

director 감독, 지도자

age 나이

activity 활동

1 I don't have any flour <u>to baked</u> bread. → _____

2 He was happy <u>to seeing</u> her there. → _____

3 He decided <u>to not</u> leave this town. → _____

4 His new job is <u>to cleaning</u> the street. → _____

5 My dream is <u>to is</u> a famous artist. → _____

6 To drink milk <u>are</u> good for your health. → _____

7 She didn't know what <u>to doing</u>. → _____

8 Ann knows good ways <u>save</u> things. → _____

9 I went to the park <u>to met</u> Lucy. → _____

10 Tom wants <u>to is</u> a movie director. → _____

11 I learned <u>swim</u> first at the age of six. → _____

12 We were sorry <u>to heard</u> the news. → _____

13 I hope <u>traveling</u> around the world. → _____

14 Who taught you how <u>to driving</u>? → _____

15 My favorite activity is <u>to took</u> a walk. → _____

16 <u>That</u> is hard to exercise every day. → _____

to부정사 · **27**

다음 우리말과 같도록 주어진 단어를 이용하여 문장을 완성하세요.

climb 오르다
cruise 유람선
designer 디자이너

1 그의 취미는 산을 오르는 것이다. (climb)

→ His hobby _____ the mountain.

2 우리는 크루즈 여행을 가는 것을 원하지 않는다. (go)

→ We don't _____ on a cruise trip.

3 Sam은 나에게 그 기계 사용하는 방법을 알려주었다. (use)

→ Sam showed me _____ the machine.

4 David는 저 차를 살 돈이 없다. (buy)

→ David has no _____ that car.

5 그녀는 파티에서 그를 보고 놀랐다. (see)

→ She was _____ him at the party.

6 Kate의 꿈은 디자이너가 되는 것이다. (become)

→ Kate's dream _____ a designer.

7 그들은 그녀에게 언제 런던으로 이사할지 물었다. (move)

→ They asked her _____ to London.

8 Susan은 뉴스를 듣기 위해 라디오를 켰다. (listen)

→ Susan turned on the _____ to the news.

9 수박을 둘로 자르는 것은 어렵다. (cut)

→ It is _____ a watermelon in half.

10 Jonathan은 놀 친구들이 많다. (play)

→ Jonathan has many _____ with.

다음 두 문장을 한 문장으로 만들어 보세요.

rumor 소문
magazine 잡지
receive 받다

1 I was very surprised. I heard the news.
   → I was very surprised to _____

2 He must be a fool. Because he believes the rumor.
   → _____

3 He went to the store. He wanted to buy a bike.
   → _____

4 Lisa went to Canada. She wanted to learn English.
   → _____

5 Cathy bought a magazine. She will read it.
   → _____

6 Tom drove to my school. He wanted to pick me up.
   → _____

7 They were glad. They received a letter from him.
   → _____

8 I need a new shirt. I want to put it on.
   → _____

9 Don't eat late at night. It is bad for your health.
   → _____

10 Bill has many books. He will read them this week.
   → _____

[1~3] 다음 중 빈칸에 알맞은 말을 고르세요.

1 He taught me _____ a car.
  ① drive
  ② drove
  ③ how drive to
  ④ how to drive

2 She has no a house to live _____.
  ① in
  ② at
  ③ on
  ④ with

3 It is not good _____ promises.
  ① break
  ② broke
  ③ to break
  ④ to breaking

4 다음 밑줄 친 부분이 어법상 어색한 것을 고르세요.
  The boy ① has ② a lot of ③ questions ④ ask me.

[5~6] 다음 중 밑줄 친 부분의 쓰임이 다른 하나를 고르세요.

5 ① I was happy to see her there.
  ② I want some water to drink.
  ③ He walked fast to go home early.
  ④ We were glad to see you again.

6 ① I want to be a doctor.
  ② My wish is to have a pet.
  ③ I went to the store to buy milk.
  ④ To talk with them is a lot of fun.

7 다음 우리말을 참고하여 not이 들어가기에 알맞은 곳을 고르세요.

  > 그 소년들은 다시는 싸우지 않겠다고 동의했다.

  The boys ① agreed ② to ③ fight ④ again.

[8~9] 다음 괄호 안의 동사를 알맞게 바꾼 것을 고르세요.

8 It is easy (solve) the question.
  ① solve
  ② solves
  ③ to solve
  ④ to sloving

9 Neil Armstrong was the first man (walk) on the moon.
  ① walk
  ② to walk
  ③ walking
  ④ how walk

[10~11] 다음 두 문장을 to부정사를 이용하여 한 문장으로 쓰세요.

10 She went to the store. She wanted to buy some fruit.
  → She went to the store _____ _____.

11 Ann was surprised. She saw someone in the dark.
  → Ann was _____.

12 다음 우리말을 영어로 바르게 옮긴 것을 고르세요.

> 외국어를 배우는 것은 어렵다.

① Learn a foreign language is hard.
② Learns a foreign language is hard.
③ To learn a foreign language is hard.
④ It is hard learn a foreign language.

13 다음 중 대화의 빈칸에 알맞은 것을 고르세요.

> A: What do you think of the news?
> B: I am very sad _____ that.

① to hear   ② hear
③ heard   ④ hearing

14 다음 밑줄 친 it의 쓰임이 다른 하나를 고르세요.

① <u>It</u> is fun to play chess.
② <u>It</u> is rainy a lot in summer.
③ <u>It</u> is difficult to walk all day long.
④ <u>It</u> is easy to spell English words.

[15~17] 다음 중 어법상 잘못된 것을 고르세요.

15 ① I have something show you.
② He wanted to believe the story.
③ There is nothing to watch on TV.
④ Please give me a pen to write with.

16 ① My dad told me what to do.
② I didn't know where to go first.
③ Please tell me when to leave here.
④ She taught me how make a pie.

17 ① I had many things to do yesterday.
② He was pleased won the race.
③ I don't have time to cook today.
④ Her hobby is to work in the garden.

18 다음 중 어법상 알맞은 문장을 고르세요.

① I like to play the piano.
② Play soccer is interesting.
③ Kate wanted to bought books.
④ My hobby is collects coins.

19 다음 우리말과 같도록 빈칸에 알맞은 말을 쓰세요.

그는 같이 놀 친구가 많았다.
= He had many friends _____ _____ _____.

20 다음 중 〈보기〉의 밑줄 친 부분과 쓰임이 같은 것을 고르세요.

> 〈보기〉 To see is <u>to believe</u>.

① I went there <u>to meet</u> my brother.
② He eats fast food <u>to save</u> time.
③ It is time <u>to go</u> to bed.
④ My dream is <u>to sing</u> on the stage.

A 다음 그림을 보고, 감정에 알맞은 내용을 찾아 완성하세요.

1	2	3

angry	sad	glad

say goodbye to him   find a bug in the soup   receive many flowers

1 I was _____

2 I was _____

3 I was _____

B 다음 그래프를 보고, 주어진 단어를 이용하여 문장을 완성하세요.

<Students' Wishes>

get better grades

become healthier

make new friends

1　2　3

1 Nine students _____.
   (hope)

2 Six students _____.
   (wish)

3 Three students _____.
   (want)

Unit 2

동명사

동명사의 의미와 쓰임을 이해하고 활용할 수 있다.

동명사를 목적어로 쓰는 동사를 알고 활용할 수 있다.

to부정사를 목적어로 쓰는 동사를 알고 활용할 수 있다.

동명사는 동사로 만든 명사형으로 동사이면서 명사 역할을 해요. 동사 끝에 -ing를 붙여서 만들며 문장에서 명사처럼 쓰여서 주어, 목적어, 보어로 쓰여요. to부정사와 비슷하지만, to부정사처럼 다양한 역할을 하지 않고 명사 역할만 해요.

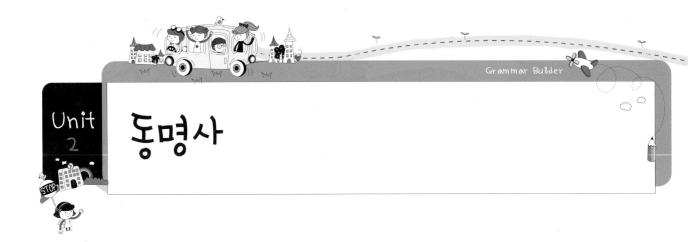

Unit 2

동명사

1. 동명사의 의미

동사이면서 명사의 역할을 한다고 해서 동명사라고 하며, 형태는 동사 뒤에 -ing를 붙인다.

• 동명사는 to부정사의 명사적 쓰임처럼 명사 역할을 한다.

• 동명사는 문장에서 주어, 목적어, 보어로 쓰인다.

동명사(동사원형 -ing)	~하기, ~하는 것	주어, 목적어, 보어로 쓰임

Playing soccer is fun. 축구하는 것은 재미있다. [주어]

I enjoy playing soccer. 나는 축구하는 것을 즐긴다. [목적어]

My hobby is playing soccer. 나의 취미는 축구이다. [보어]

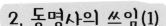

동명사는 문장에서
to부정사처럼
다양한 역할을 하지 않고
명사의 역할만 한다.

2. 동명사의 쓰임(1)

(1) 주어 역할을 할 때는 '~하는 것은'으로 해석하고 단수 취급한다.

Eating vegetables is good for your health. 야채를 먹는 것은 건강에 좋다.

Making good friends is important. 좋은 친구를 사귀는 것이 중요하다.

→ To make good friends is important.

→ It is important to make good friends.

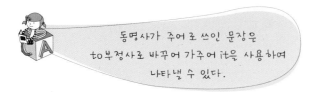

동명사가 주어로 쓰인 문장은
to부정사로 바꾸어 가주어 it을 사용하여
나타낼 수 있다.

(2) 동명사가 보어 역할을 할 때는 '~하는 것이다'로 해석한다.

My hobby is collecting coins. 나의 취미는 동전을 모으는 것이다.

→ My hobby is to collect coins.

동명사가
보어로 쓰인 문장도
to부정사로 바꾸어
나타낼 수 있다.

(3) 동명사는 to부정사의 명사적 역할에 없는 전치사의 목적어 역할도 한다.

Thank you for calling me.

나에게 전화해 줘서 고마워.

전치사 뒤에는 명사가 오는데,
동사가 올 경우에는 동명사의 형태로 쓴다.

Pop Quiz

I. 다음 괄호 안에서 알맞은 것을 고르세요.

❶ (Play, Playing) the piano is fun.

❷ Thank you for (help, helping) me.

3. 동명사의 쓰임(2)

동사의 종류에 따라 동명사를 목적어로 쓰거나, to부정사를 목적어로 쓴다.

(1) 동명사만 쓰는 동사

enjoy 즐기다, finish 끝마치다, give up 포기하다,
stop 그만두다, postpone 연기하다, admit 인정하다,
avoid 피하다, imagine 상상하다, consider 고려하다,
keep 계속하다

stop은
목적어로 동명사를 쓰며,
뒤에 to부정사가 오면
부사적 쓰임(목적)이다.

I finished doing my homework. 나는 나의 숙제를 끝마쳤다.

She enjoys jogging. 그녀는 조깅을 즐긴다.

He stopped singing. 그는 노래 부르는 것을 멈췄다.

He stopped to sing.
그는 노래를 부르기 위해 멈췄다.

(2) to부정사만 쓰는 동사

> want 원하다, plan 계획하다, hope 희망하다, decide 결정하다, offer 제안하다,
> promise 약속하다, agree 동의하다, learn 배우다, forget 잊다, fail 실패하다

We decided to take a walk. 우리는 산책을 하기로 결정했다.

I agreed to help him. 나는 그를 돕기로 동의했다.

They want to go to Jeju-do. 그들은 제주도에 가기를 원한다.

(3) 동명사와 to부정사 모두 쓰는 동사

> like 좋아하다, love 사랑하다, begin 시작하다, hate 싫어하다,
> start 시작하다, continue 계속하다, bother 괴롭히다

It started raining. = It started to rain. 비가 오기 시작했다.

I like reading books. = I like to read books. 나는 책 읽기를 좋아한다.

We continued working. = We continued to work. 우리는 일을 계속했다.

(4) 동명사와 to부정사 모두 쓰지만 의미가 달라지는 동사

> remember -ing: ~했던 것을 기억하다, remember to부정사: ~해야 하는 것을 기억하다,
> regret -ing: ~했던 것을 후회하다, regret to부정사: ~해야 해서 유감이다

I remember locking the door. 나는 그 문을 닫았던 것을 기억한다.

Remember to lock the door. 그 문을 잠가야 하는 것을 기억해라.

He regrets wearing the coat. 그는 그 코트 입은 것을 후회한다.

She regrets to say that. 그녀는 그것을 말해야 해서 유감이다.

> **Pop Quiz** 2. 다음 괄호 안에서 알맞은 것을 고르세요.
> ❶ I want (to dance, dancing).
> ❷ He finished (to do, doing) the work.

다음 문장에서 동명사에 동그라미 하세요.

stamp 우표
afraid 두려워하는
avoid 피하다

1 Sending an e-mail is not difficult.

2 His hobby is collecting stamps.

3 Amy hates talking with others.

4 The kid finished doing his homework.

5 Thank you for inviting me.

6 Playing baseball is very interesting.

7 They like taking pictures.

8 Learning English is very useful.

9 I stopped watching the movie.

10 It starts snowing at that time.

11 Driving fast is dangerous.

12 Sally is afraid of flying on plane.

13 My dream is opening a bakery.

14 He avoids drinking soda because it's bad.

15 My mother enjoys cooking in the kitchen.

16 I am good at speaking French.

다음 괄호 안에서 알맞은 것을 골라 동그라미 하세요.

surf 서핑을 하다
continue 계속하다
diary 일기
nervous 불안한
imagine 상상하다

1   His hobby is (surf, surfing) the Internet.

2   He continued (read, to read) the books.

3   Thank you for (calling, to call) me.

4   Jenny gave up (taking, to take) the math test.

5   My job is (selling, sell) cars.

6   How about (to jog, jogging) in the morning?

7   The boy stopped (to watch, watch) TV.

8   We hope (to meet, meeting) Lisa soon.

9   (Keep, Keeping) a diary is not boring.

10   They enjoyed (to ride, riding) the roller coaster.

11   I agreed (to help, helping) her yesterday.

12   They talked about (take, taking) a trip.

13   He is nervous about (meeting, meet) new people.

14   We didn't imagine (to see, seeing) you here.

15   When did you learn (swimming, to swim)?

16   Ann and Tom are sorry for (to be, being) late.

다음 괄호 안에서 알맞은 것을 골라 동그라미 하세요.

1 She admitted (making, make) a mistake.

2 He offered (to go, going) to the mountain.

3 Ann avoided (to answer, answering) my question.

4 They promised not (being, to be) late for school.

5 She wants (eating, to eat) spaghetti.

6 We gave up (having, to have) dinner.

7 I am considering (living, live) in a country.

8 He postponed (to do, doing) his work.

9 I often imagine (travel, traveling) around the world.

10 We decided (helping, to help) the children.

11 (Stand, Standing) all day is not easy.

12 I didn't enjoy (taking, to take) a walk.

13 I finished (cleaning, to clean) my room.

14 I hope (going, to go) to see a movie.

15 Kate failed (passing, to pass) the exam.

16 She plans (to go, going) abroad next month.

admit 인정하다
consider 고려하다
postpone 연기하다
exam 시험

다음 빈칸에 주어진 동사를 알맞은 형태로 쓰세요.

ski 스키를 타다
proud 자랑스러운
horse 말

1 Matt decided _____ a house. (buy)

2 The man admitted _____ the money. (steal)

3 Bob is good at _____. (ski)

4 Do you finish _____ the novel? (read)

5 Jill doesn't give up _____ a job. (get)

6 They postponed _____ the wall. (paint)

7 He learned _____ a computer. (use)

8 Don't forget _____ a letter. (send, ~할 것을 잊다)

9 He is proud of _____ a lawyer. (be)

10 He and she wanted _____ in the pool. (swim)

11 They plan _____ to Europe next week. (go)

12 Mike failed _____ a hotel to stay. (find)

13 I remember _____ the door. (lock, ~했던 것을 기억하다)

14 I enjoyed _____ a horse in the field. (ride)

15 Are you interested in _____ the movie? (watch)

16 Ashley considered _____ him again. (meet)

다음 빈칸에 주어진 동사를 알맞은 형태로 쓰세요.

midnight 한밤중
another 다른
business 사업
neighbor 이웃

1 Cathy finished _____ at midnight. (study)

2 The kids offered _____ the car. (wash)

3 They enjoyed _____ with the dolls. (play)

4 Does he love _____ a kite? (fly)

5 It stopped _____ a few minutes ago. (rain)

6 Jane can't avoid _____ the question. (answer)

7 Lucy wanted _____ with them. (come)

8 He stopped _____ five years ago. (smoke)

9 We decided _____ here yesterday. (leave)

10 The boy admitted _____ the vase. (break)

11 The children kept _____ for their friend. (wait)

12 Thank you for _____ me at the party. (invite)

13 Jack hoped _____ for another job. (look)

14 Finally, I gave up _____ for the exam. (prepare)

15 The people talked about _____ a business. (open)

16 His neighbor started _____ cookies. (make)

다음 빈칸에 주어진 동사를 알맞은 형태로 쓰세요.

lake 호수
sneaker 운동화
line 선
cough 기침을 하다

1 Please stop _____ in the lake. (swim)

2 They avoided _____ in winter. (travel)

3 Why do you keep _____ me questions? (ask)

4 Sally wants _____ the sneakers. (buy)

5 We are considering _____ to Seoul. (move)

6 When did he learn _____ the cello? (play)

7 Brian postponed _____ her phone. (answer)

8 My cat is good at _____. (hide)

9 The man promised _____ on time. (be)

10 People need _____ in line. (stand)

11 I have a bad cold. I can't stop _____. (cough)

12 Mark wants _____ your house some day. (visit)

13 She gave up _____ to the party. (go)

14 I'm worried about _____ late for school. (be)

15 I decided _____ for him for one more hour. (wait)

16 Peter began _____ the thick book. (read)

다음 우리말과 같도록 주어진 단어를 이용하여 문장을 완성하세요.

diary 일기
future 미래

1 그는 나의 질문에 답하는 것을 피했다. (avoid, answer)

He _____ my question.

2 그때 비가 오기 시작했다. (start, rain)

It _____ at that time.

3 나는 나의 오랜 친구를 만나서 행복했다. (happy, meet)

I was _____ my old friend.

4 그녀의 좋은 습관은 아침에 일찍 일어나는 것이다. (is, get)

Her good habit _____ up early in the morning.

5 너는 미래에 무엇을 하고 싶니? (do, like)

What would you _____ in the future?

6 그 남자는 그 사무실에서 계속 일을 했다. (continue, work)

The man _____ in the office.

7 Lisa는 약간의 꽃을 사기 위해 가게에 갔다. (buy, shop)

Lisa went to a _____ some flowers.

8 나의 취미는 피아노를 연주하는 것이다. (is, play)

My hobby _____ the piano.

9 그들은 그 친구를 보기 위해 병원에 갔다. (hospital, see)

They went to the _____ the friend.

10 그 어린이는 일기를 쓰기로 결정했다.

The children _____ a diary. (decide, keep)

11 그는 그 도시로 이사하는 것을 고려했다. (consider, move)

He _____ to the city.

동명사 · **43**

다음 우리말과 같도록 주어진 단어를 이용하여 문장을 완성하세요.

director 감독
bake 굽다
stage 무대

1 그는 종일 그의 개를 찾는 것을 계속했다. (keep, look for)

→ He _____ his dog all day.

2 그 아기는 밤에 울기 시작했다. (begin, cry)

→ The baby _____ at night.

3 그들은 그 창문을 깬 것을 인정했다. (break, admit)

→ They _____ the window.

4 나는 자동차를 운전하는 것을 즐기지 않는다. (enjoy, drive)

→ I don't _____ a car.

5 그는 영화 감독이 되어 싶어한다. (is, want)

→ He _____ a movie director.

6 Tom과 Dan은 수학 공부하는 것을 싫어한다. (hate, study)

→ Tom and Dan _____ math.

7 Amy는 모형 차 만드는 것을 포기했다. (give up, make)

→ Amy _____ a model car.

8 우리는 약간의 쿠키를 굽기로 결정했다. (decide, bake)

→ We _____ some cookies.

9 그는 무대에서 춤추는 것을 멈추었다. (dance, stop)

→ He _____ on the stage.

10 나는 언젠가 백두산을 오르기를 희망한다. (hope, climb)

→ I _____ Mt. Baekdu someday.

11 Julia는 영어로 편지 쓰는 것을 매우 좋아한다. (love, write)

→ Julia _____ a letter in English.

다음 빈칸에 알맞은 말을 〈보기〉에서 골라 알맞은 형태로 쓰세요.

useful 유용한
mirror 거울
culture 문화
weight 무게

| 〈보기〉 | lose | close | talk | plant | cook | play | ride |
| | meet | read | go | save | learn | break | invite |

I Sally enjoys _____ pizza for lunch.

2 Do you want _____ the window?

3 _____ your money is important.

4 My dad planned _____ flowers in the garden.

5 Thank you for _____ us at the party.

6 Tim and Thomas are good at _____ tennis.

7 She offered _____ him at the cafe.

8 We decided _____ abroad next month.

9 _____ a bike is very fun.

10 _____ English is useful.

II The kid admitted _____ the mirror.

12 Kate's hobby is _____ novels.

13 Peter continued _____ about the culture.

14 Tony gave up _____ weight.

다음 빈칸에 알맞은 말을 쓰세요.

1 동사면서 명사 역할을 한다고 해서 _____ 라고 하며, 형태는 동사 뒤에 - _____ 를 붙인다.

2 동명사는 문장에서 to부정사처럼 다양한 역할을 하지 않고 _____ 역할을 하며, 문장에서 주어, _____, 보어로 쓰인다.

3 동명사가 주어 역할을 할 때는 '~ _____ '으로 해석하고 _____ 취급한다. 또한 동명사가 주어로 쓰인 문장은 to부정사로 바꾸어 가주어 _____ 을 사용하여 나타낼 수 있다.

4 전치사 뒤에는 명사가 오는데, 동사가 올 경우에는 _____ 의 형태로 쓴다.

5 enjoy, finish, stop, give up, postpone, avoid 등의 동사는 동명사와 to부정사 중에 목적어로 _____ 만을 쓴다.

6 want, plan, hope, decide, agree 등의 동사는 동명사와 to부정사 중에 목적어로 _____ 만을 쓴다.

7 like, love, begin, start, continue 등의 동사는 동명사와 to부정사 중에 목적어로 _____ 와 _____ 를 모두 쓴다.

8 remember -ing는 ' _____ (과거)', remember to부정사는 '~해야 하는 것을 기억하다(미래)'라는 뜻이다.

다음 문장에서 밑줄 친 부분을 바르게 고쳐 쓰세요.

pack 꾸리다, 싸다
nail 손톱
speech 연설

1   Keep a diary is not easy.   → _____

2   He and she consider move to Seoul. → _____

3   Thank you for come with me.   → _____

4   They decided met you again.   → _____

5   He hates to talking with new people. → _____

6   We enjoy take a walk in the evening. → _____

7   He promised not being late again. → _____

8   We finish to pack these bags.   → _____

9   Mark is afraid of swim in the lake. → _____

10 His bad habit is to bites his nails. → _____

11 Alice postponed to visit her uncle. → _____

12 She is worried about make a speech. → _____

13 Jonathan wants losing some weight. → _____

14 Eric and Bob agreed not fight again. → _____

15 The girl hates to wearing a skirt. → _____

16 The man never gave up to find a job. → _____

다음 우리말과 같도록 괄호 안의 말을 알맞게 배열하세요.

important 중요한
town 마을
gallery 미술관

1 컴퓨터를 배우는 것은 어렵지 않다.
(a computer, not, difficult, learning, is)
→ _____

2 그녀는 쿠키 만드는 것을 포기하지 않았다.
(she, give up, cookies, didn't, making)
→ _____

3 병들을 재활용하는 것은 매우 중요하다.
(recycling, is, very, bottles, important)
→ _____

4 Thomas는 그 마을을 떠나기로 결정했다.
(Thomas, the town, decided, to leave)
→ _____

5 깊은 물에서 수영하는 것은 위험하다.
(dangerous, in, is, swimming, the deep water)
→ _____

6 TV를 너무 많이 보는 것은 좋지 않다.
(is, not, too much, good, watching, TV)
→ _____

7 영어로 연설하는 것은 쉽다.
(in English, making, is, a speech, easy)
→ _____

8 그 어린이들은 미술관에 가기를 희망한다.
(hope, to the gallery, the children, to go)
→ _____

다음 우리말과 같도록 빈칸에 알맞은 말을 쓰세요.

scientist 과학자
fishbowl 어항
picnic 소풍
wallet 지갑

1 그는 위대한 과학자가 되고 싶어한다.
→ He wants _____ _____ a great scientist.

2 그는 새 직업을 구하는 것을 포기하지 않았다.
→ He didn't _____ _____ getting a new job.

3 그 커플은 시골로 이사하기로 결정했다.
→ The couple decided _____ _____ to a country.

4 Brian은 그 어항을 깬 것을 인정했다.
→ Brian admitted _____ _____ the fishbowl.

5 나의 취미는 기타를 연주하는 것이다.
→ My hobby _____ _____ the guitar.

6 그 남자는 그 기계를 사용하는 것을 배웠다.
→ The man learned _____ _____ the machine.

7 우리는 소풍 가는 것을 계획하고 있다.
→ We are planning _____ _____ on a picnic.

8 그녀는 그녀의 숙제하는 것을 미룬다.
→ She postpones _____ her homework.

9 그 소녀는 그녀의 지갑을 계속 찾았다.
→ The girl continued _____ her wallet.

10 그들은 그때 그를 돕는 것을 동의했다.
→ They agreed _____ _____ him at that time.

11 수영을 하는 것은 너의 건강에 매우 좋다.
→ _____ _____ very good for your health.

[1~3] 다음 중 문장의 빈칸에 알맞은 말을 고르세요.

1 _____ baseball is very fun.
① Play   ② Plays
③ Playing   ④ To playing

2 I considered _____ in a country.
① live   ② living
③ lived   ④ to live

3 Thank you for _____ me.
① call   ② to call
③ to calling ④ calling

[4~5] 빈칸에 알맞지 <u>않은</u> 것을 고르세요.

4 Lucy _____ to lose some weight.
① avoided   ② needs
③ is planning ④ hopes

5 Do you _____ keeping a diary in English?
① finish   ② postpone
③ start   ④ wish

6 다음 빈칸에 알맞은 말을 괄호 안에 주어진 동사를 이용하여 쓰세요.

> John admitted _____ the bottle. (break)

→ _____

7 다음 밑줄 친 부분을 바르게 고친 것을 고르세요.

> Peter decided <u>buy</u> the car.

① buy   ② to buy
③ buying   ④ 고칠 필요 없음.

[8~9] 다음 중 우리말을 영어로 바르게 옮긴 것을 고르세요.

8 Cathy는 영어를 잘한다.
① Cathy is good at speaking English.
② Cathy is good at speak English.
③ Cathy is good to speaking English.
④ Cathy is good to speak English.

9 우리는 그를 돕기로 약속했다.
① We promised help him.
② We promised helping him.
③ We promised to help him.
④ We promised to helping him.

10 다음 빈칸에 들어갈 말이 알맞게 짝지어진 것을 고르세요.

> · They gave up _____ breakfast.
> · Jonathan failed _____ the test.

① have – pass
② having – to pass
③ having – passing
④ to have – to pass

11 다음 빈칸에 공통으로 들어가기에 알맞은 것을 고르세요.

> · My hobby is _____ on the Internet.
> · I enjoy _____ about my school life.

① write ② wrote
③ writing ④ to write

12 다음 중 빈칸에 playing이 들어갈 수 <u>없는</u> 것을 고르세요.

① Ann wants _____ the piano.
② We like _____ soccer after school.
③ His hobby is _____ the guitar.
④ The kid stops _____ with the dolls.

13 다음 밑줄 친 부분 중 어법상 <u>어색한</u> 것을 고르세요.

I was ① <u>worried about</u> ② <u>making the</u> speech. So I ③ <u>continued</u> ④ <u>practice</u> the speech.

14 다음 우리말과 같도록 빈칸에 들어갈 수 있는 것을 모두 고르세요.

> Amy는 한국 음식을 요리하는 것을 매우 좋아한다.
> = Amy loves _____ Korean food.

① cook ② cooking
③ to cook ④ cooked

15 다음 빈칸에 공통으로 들어갈 말로 알맞지 <u>않은</u> 것을 고르세요.

> · Jane and her sister _____ playing the game.
> · Joe and his friend _____ to listen to the radio.

① want ② love
③ begin ④ like

[16~17] 다음 중 어법상 올바른 문장을 고르세요.

16 ① Sam finished to do his homework.
② They didn't imagine to meet her here.
③ Sally offers to write the letter.
④ He avoided to answer my question.

17 ① We planed going abroad next week.
② Send an e-mail is not difficult.
③ Matt hopes meeting Lisa tomorrow.
④ The old woman learned to drive a car.

18 다음 문장에서 어법상 <u>어색한</u> 부분을 찾아 고쳐 쓰세요.

> My brother is afraid of skate on the ice.

_____ → _____

A 다음 괄호 안의 말을 이용하여 〈보기〉와 같이 문장을 바꾸세요.

〈보기〉 He watches TV in the living room. (enjoy)
→ He enjoys watching TV in the living room.

1 We did our homework yesterday. (finish)

→ _____

2 She finds a four-leaf clover in the garden. (hope)

→ _____

3 Sally tried to go on a diet during the vacation. (give up)

→ _____

B 다음 Thomas를 소개하는 메모를 보고, 문장을 완성하세요.

이름: Thomas
취미: 음악 감상, 책 읽기
특기: 모형 자동차 만들기
좋아하는 것: 애완견과 함께 놀기
싫어하는 것: 일찍 일어나기

My name is Thomas. Let me introduce myself.

1 My hobbies are _____ and _____.

2 I am good at _____.

3 I enjoy _____. But I hate _____.

현재분사와 과거분사

현재분사의 형태와 쓰임을 이해하고 활용할 수 있다.

과거분사의 형태와 쓰임을 이해하고 활용할 수 있다.

분사는 동사에서 갈라져 나온 말이라는 뜻에서 붙여진 이름으로, 동사 뒤에 -ing를 붙여 현재분사가 되면 능동적이고 진행적인 뜻을 갖게 돼요. 그 뒤에 -ed를 붙여 과거분사가 되면 수동적이고 완료적인 뜻을 갖게 돼요. 분사들은 형용사처럼 쓰여서 명사를 수식하거나 주어와 목적어의 상태를 나타내는 보어로 쓰여요.

Unit 3

현재분사와 과거분사

1. 현재분사의 형태와 쓰임

현재분사는 〈동사원형＋-ing〉의 형태로, '~하는, ~하고 있는'의 뜻으로 능동과 진행을 나타낸다.

• 형태: 〈동사원형＋-ing〉

(1) be동사와 함께 쓰여 진행형을 만든다.

He is cleaning the room now. 그는 지금 그 방을 청소하고 있다.

The children were playing soccer. 그 어린이들은 축구를 하고 있었다.

(2) 명사 앞이나 뒤에서 형용사처럼 명사를 수식한다.

The smiling baby is cute. 웃고 있는 아기는 귀엽다.

The baby smiling on the bed is cute. 침대에서 웃고 있는 아기는 귀엽다.

명사 앞에서 수식하지만,
수식어구와 함께 쓰이면
명사 뒤에서 수식한다.

(3) 주어나 목적어의 상태를 설명하는 보어 역할을 한다.

I saw him singing on the stage. 나는 무대에서 노래를 부르는 그를 보았다.

2. 과거분사의 형태와 쓰임

과거분사는 〈동사원형＋-ed〉 또는 〈불규칙 변화〉 형태로, '~된, ~받는'의 뜻으로 수동과 완료를 나타낸다.

• 형태: 〈동사원형＋-ed〉 또는 〈불규칙 변화〉

(1) 명사 앞이나 뒤에서 형용사처럼 명사를 수식한다.

Look at the broken window. 그 깨진 창문을 보아라.

I saw the mountain covered with snow. 나는 눈으로 덮인 산을 보았다.

(2) 주어나 목적어의 상태를 설명하는 보어 역할을 한다.

I found the letter written in English. 나는 영어로 쓰여진 편지를 발견했다.

Pop Quiz 1. 다음 괄호 안의 분사가 들어갈 곳을 고르세요.

❶ Look at ① the ② birds. (flying)

❷ He found ① his ② watch. (stolen)

3. 감정을 나타내는 분사

surprise, interest, excite 등 사람의 감정을 나타낸 동사가 현재분사나 과거분사로 쓰여 문장에서
형용사 역할을 한다.

• 현재분사는 주어가 감정의 원인이 되는 것을 유발할 때 쓰인다.

• 과거분사는 주로 사람을 주어로 하여 느끼는 감정을 나타낸다.

현재분사 ~하게 하는	surprising 놀라운	interesting 재미있는	boring 지루한	exciting 흥분시키는	shocking 충격적인
과거분사 ~하게 된	surprised 놀란	interested 재미를 느끼는	bored 지루해진	excited 흥분된	shocked 충격 받은

The news was very surprising. 그 뉴스는 매우 놀라웠다.

They were surprised at the news. 그들은 그 소식에 놀랐다.

주로 현재분사는 사물이 주어이거나 사물을 수식할 때,
과거분사는 사람이 주어이거나 사람을 수식할 때 쓰인다.
하지만 항상 그런 것은 아니다.

4. 현재분사와 동명사의 구별

현재분사와 동명사는 둘 다 〈동사원형＋-ing〉의 형태이지만 쓰임은 다르다.

- 현재분사: 문장에서 형용사 역할(명사 수식)과 서술적 역할(진행형)
- 동명사: 문장에서 명사 역할(주어, 목적어, 보어로 쓰임)

	현재분사	동명사
형태	동사원형＋-ing	동사원형＋-ing
역할	형용사 역할, 서술적 역할	명사 역할(주어, 목적어, 보어)
의미	~하는, ~하고 있는	~하는 것, ~하기

The sleeping baby is my cousin. [현재분사] 그 자고 있는 아기는 나의 사촌이다.

Sleeping in the tent is fun. [동명사] 텐트에서 자는 것은 재미있다.

She is taking pictures there. [현재분사] 그녀는 거기서 사진을 찍고 있다.

Her hobby is taking pictures. [동명사] 그녀의 취미는 사진을 찍는 것이다.

Pop Quiz 2. 다음 괄호 안에서 알맞은 것을 고르세요.
❶ The book is (boring, bored).
❷ The (exciting, excited) man shouted.

불규칙 동사 변화표

현재	과거	과거분사	현재	과거	과거분사
am, is/are ~이다	was/were	been	fight 싸우다	fought	fought
become 되다	became	became	find 발견하다	found	found
begin 시작하다	began	begun	fly 날다	flew	flown
bite 물다	bit	bitten	forget 잊다	forgot	forgotten
break 깨다	broke	broken	forgive 용서하다	forgave	forgiven
bring 가져오다	brought	brought	freeze 얼다	froze	frozen
build 짓다	built	built	get 얻다	got	got/gotten
burn 타다	burned/burnt	burned/burnt	give 주다	gave	given
buy 사다	bought	bought	go 가다	went	gone
catch 잡다	caught	caught	grow 자라다	grew	grown
choose 선택하다	chose	chose	hang 걸다	hung	hung
cost 가격이 들다	cost	cost	have 가지다, 먹다	had	had
come 오다	came	come	hear 듣다	heard	heard
cut 자르다	cut	cut	hide 숨다	hid	hidden
do 하다	did	done	hit 치다	hit	hit
draw 그리다	drew	drawn	hold 잡다	held	held
drink 마시다	drank	drunk	hurt 다치게하다	hurt	hurt
drive 운전하다	drove	driven	keep 유지하다	kept	kept
eat 먹다	ate	eaten	know 알다	knew	known
fall 떨어지다	fell	fallen	lay 놓다	laid	laid
feed 먹이를 주다	fed	fed	leave 떠나다	left	left
feel 느끼다	felt	felt	lend 빌려주다	lent	lent

현재	과거	과거분사	현재	과거	과거분사
let ~하게 하다	let	let	shut 닫다	shut	shut
lie 거짓말하다	lied	lied	sing 노래하다	sang	sung
lie 눕다	lay	lay	sit 앉다	sat	sat
lose 지다	lost	lost	sleep 자다	slept	slept
make 만들다	made	made	speak 말하다	spoke	spoken
mean 의미하다	meant	meant	spend 쓰다	spent	spent
meet 만나다	met	met	stand 서 있다	stood	stood
pay 지불하다	paid	paid	steal 훔치다	stole	stolen
put 놓다, 두다	put	put	swim 수영하다	swam	swum
quit 그만두다	quit	quit	take 잡다	took	taken
read 읽다	read	read	teach 가르치다	taught	taught
ride 타다	rode	ridden	tear 찢다	tore	torn
ring 소리가 울리다	rang	rung	tell 말하다	told	told
rise 일어나다	rose	risen	think 생각하다	thought	thought
run 달리다	ran	run	throw 던지다	threw	thrown
say 말하다	said	said	understand 이해하다	understood	understood
see 보다	saw	seen	wake 깨우다	woke	woken
sell 팔다	sold	sold	wear 입다	wore	worn
send 보내다	sent	sent	win 이기다	won	won
set 놓다, 두다	set	set	write 쓰다	wrote	written

 **Check Up 1**

다음 동사의 현재분사와 과거분사를 골라 동그라미 하세요.

1 walk – (walkking, **walking**) – (walkked, **walked**)

2 hit – (**hitting**, hiting) – (hitted, **hit**)

3 smile – (smileing, **smiling**) – (**smiled**, smileed)

4 stop – (stoping, **stopping**) – (stoped, **stopped**)

5 bring – (bring, **bringing**) – (**brought**, bringed)

6 have – (**having**, haveing) – (**had**, haved)

7 read – (readding, **reading**) – (**read**, readed)

8 play – (plaiing, **playing**) – (plaied, **played**)

9 go – (**going**, gooing) – (**gone**, went)

10 dance – (**dancing**, danceing) – (**danced**, dancen)

11 plan – (planing, **planning**) – (planed, **planned**)

12 think – (**thinking**, thinkking) – (**thought**, thinked)

13 give – (giveing, **giving**) – (**given**, gave)

14 open – (openning, **opening**) – (openned, **opened**)

15 buy – (buiing, **buying**) – (**bought**, buyed)

16 eat – (**eating**, eatting) – (**eaten**, ate)

다음 빈칸에 동사의 과거분사 형태를 쓰세요.

1 study	_____	**2** sleep	_____
3 let	_____	**4** understand	_____
5 stay	_____	**6** throw	_____
7 wash	_____	**8** put	_____
9 bite	_____	**10** forget	_____
11 make	_____	**12** visit	_____
13 mean	_____	**14** speak	_____
15 listen	_____	**16** say	_____
17 pay	_____	**18** stand	_____
19 plan	_____	**20** steal	_____
21 stop	_____	**22** have	_____
23 read	_____	**24** take	_____
25 cut	_____	**26** cover	_____
27 cry	_____	**28** dance	_____
29 rise	_____	**30** tell	_____
31 run	_____	**32** think	_____

다음 빈칸에 동사의 과거분사 형태를 쓰세요.

1 am	_____	**2** feel	_____
3 smile	_____	**4** forgive	_____
5 cost	_____	**6** shut	_____
7 worry	_____	**8** fly	_____
9 lose	_____	**10** sit	_____
11 break	_____	**12** love	_____
13 pass	_____	**14** begin	_____
15 build	_____	**16** get	_____
17 come	_____	**18** push	_____
19 feed	_____	**20** know	_____
21 quit	_____	**22** swim	_____
23 look	_____	**24** hang	_____
25 ride	_____	**26** teach	_____
27 do	_____	**28** hear	_____
29 draw	_____	**30** hide	_____
31 drink	_____	**32** hit	_____

Check Up 4

다음 빈칸에 동사의 과거분사 형태를 쓰세요.

1	lend	_____	2	set	_____
3	are	_____	4	fight	_____
5	become	_____	6	carry	_____
7	write	_____	8	sing	_____
9	fall	_____	10	keep	_____
11	play	_____	12	find	_____
13	bring	_____	14	freeze	_____
15	meet	_____	16	spend	_____
17	buy	_____	18	give	_____
19	walk	_____	20	go	_____
21	choose	_____	22	grow	_____
23	catch	_____	24	try	_____
25	send	_____	26	bake	_____
27	ring	_____	28	win	_____
29	finish	_____	30	wear	_____
31	see	_____	32	leave	_____

다음 괄호 안에서 알맞은 것을 골라 동그라미 하세요.

1 What are you (looking, looked) for?

2 The boy (talking, talk) on the phone is my brother.

3 She heard her name (calling, called) somewhere.

4 The kids are (waited, waiting) for their parents.

5 Sally studies all day. So she felt (tiring, tired).

6 We have an (interesting, interested) toy.

7 I saw the girl (crossing, crossed) the street.

8 There are many (closing, closed) stores.

9 The man (sitting, sat) on the bench is Mark.

10 They found his (losing, lost) bag.

11 Look at the dog (walking, walked) like a human.

12 This is a book (writing, written) in English.

13 I was (standing, stood) in front of the door.

14 I had cookies (covering, covered) with chocolate.

15 The girl (played, playing) the violin is my sister.

16 Some trees were (planting, planted) in the garden.

somewhere
어딘가에

cross 횡단하다

human 인간

cover 덮다

plant 심다

다음 밑줄 친 부분이 동명사인지 현재분사인지 쓰세요.

1 The children are <u>flying</u> the kites.　　(　　　　)

2 My favorite sport is <u>playing</u> tennis.　　(　　　　)

3 The <u>sleeping</u> baby is my son.　　(　　　　)

4 <u>Talking</u> with her was fun.　　(　　　　)

5 <u>Eating</u> fast food is not a healthy habit. (　　　　)

6 Many pigs are <u>rolling</u> in the mud.　　(　　　　)

7 The girl <u>sitting</u> on the sofa is pretty.　　(　　　　)

8 I started <u>studying</u> math an hour ago.　　(　　　　)

9 Look at the <u>running</u> horses.　　(　　　　)

10 Who is the boy <u>reading</u> the magazine? (　　　　)

11 Her pleasure is <u>collecting</u> coins.　　(　　　　)

12 He likes <u>watering</u> the flowers.　　(　　　　)

13 They are <u>chatting</u> at the cafe now.　　(　　　　)

14 <u>Learning</u> Chinese is not difficult.　　(　　　　)

15 His duty is <u>helping</u> the poor people.　　(　　　　)

16 She was <u>wearing</u> a wedding dress.　　(　　　　)

habit 습관
roll 구르다
pleasure 기쁨
water 물을 주다
chat 수다를 떨다
duty 의무

Step 2 **Build Up 1**

다음 괄호 안의 동사를 알맞은 형태로 바꾸어 쓰세요.

bottle 병
rope 줄
pour 붓다
cost 지출, 비용

1 Please answer the _____ question. (give)

2 Can you see the man _____ on the road? (run)

3 Look at the girl _____ a picture. (draw)

4 Don't touch the _____ bottle. (break)

5 The people were _____ the rope. (hold)

6 Do you know the _____ man? (sleep)

7 My son is _____ a bike at the park. (ride)

8 Look at the _____ leaves. (fall)

9 The _____ potatoes are delicious. (bake)

10 Bill was _____ in London then. (stay)

11 Some people _____ to the party come. (invite)

12 Pour the water over the _____ fire. (burn)

13 This is the _____ book. (borrow)

14 The cost _____ on her birthday was much. (spend)

15 Thomas is the boy _____ in Canada. (bear)

16 They called him a _____ dictionary. (walk)

다음 괄호 안의 동사를 알맞은 형태로 바꾸어 쓰세요.

Spanish 스페인어
abroad 해외로
shine 빛나다
worry 걱정하다
shade 그늘
treasure 보물

1 Look at the _____ butterfly. (fly)

2 Be careful of the _____ window. (break)

3 We know the man _____ next to the gate. (stand)

4 This book is _____ in Spanish. (write)

5 His father told us a _____ story. (interest)

6 My parents are _____ abroad now. (travel)

7 The chef served _____ fish for lunch. (cook)

8 The girl _____ in the pool is my sister. (swim)

9 Look at the stars _____ in the sky. (shine)

10 Ashley heard her name _____. (call)

11 We found Jill _____ the dishes. (wash)

12 He tried to open the _____ door. (close)

13 She took photos of the _____ babies. (smile)

14 You looked _____ about something. (worry)

15 Two men are _____ in the shade. (sleep.)

16 They found the treasure _____ in the cave. (hide)

다음 괄호 안의 동사를 알맞은 형태로 바꾸어 쓰세요.

visit 방문
score 점수
result 결과
attitude 태도
accident 사고
crowd 군중

1 She was very _____ by my visit. (surprise)

2 His behavior was _____. (disappoint)

3 John was _____ by his test score. (shock)

4 This book is very _____. (bore)

5 She is _____ in Latin dance. (interest)

6 Soccer is an _____ game. (excite)

7 That is a _____ news. (surprise)

8 Last weekend was _____. (tire)

9 Are you _____ with the result? (satisfy)

10 I had nothing to do, I was _____. (bore)

11 I don't think I will be _____. (disappoint)

12 I failed the exam so I'm _____. (depress)

13 She studied hard to get a _____ grade. (satisfy)

14 He is _____ with her changed attitude. (confuse)

15 That accident was very _____. (shock)

16 The _____ crowd shouted. (excite)

다음 빈칸에 알맞은 말을 쓰세요.

1 현재분사는 〈동사원형+-_____〉의 형태로, '~하는, ~하고 있는'의 뜻으로 능동과 _____을 나타낸다.

2 현재분사의 쓰임은

(1) be동사와 함께 쓰여 _____을 만든다.

(2) 명사 앞이나 뒤에서 형용사처럼 _____를 수식한다.

(3) 주어나 목적어의 상태를 설명하는 _____ 역할을 한다.

3 과거분사는 〈동사원형+-_____〉 또는 〈_____ 변화〉 형태로, '~받는, ~된'의 뜻으로 _____과 완료를 나타낸다.

4 과거분사의 쓰임은

(1) 명사 앞이나 뒤에서 형용사처럼 _____를 수식한다.

(2) 주어나 목적어의 상태를 설명하는 _____ 역할을 한다.

5 사람의 감정을 나타낸 동사가 분사로 쓰여 문장에서 _____ 역할을 한다.

• _____ 분사는 주어가 감정의 원인이 되는 것을 유발할 때 나타낸다.

• _____ 분사는 주로 사람을 주어로 하여 느끼는 감정을 나타낸다.

6 현재분사와 동명사는 〈동사원형+-_____〉 형태로 같지만 쓰임은 다르다.

	현재분사	동명사
형태	동사원형+-ing	동사원형+-ing
역할	_____ 역할, 서술적 역할 진행형	_____ 역할 (주어, 목적어, 보어)
의미	~하는, ~하고 있는	~하기, ~하는 것

다음 문장에서 밑줄 친 부분을 바르게 고쳐 쓰세요.

horizon 수평선
vase 꽃병
respect 존경하다
float 떠다니다
back 등
wood 목재, 나무

1 The mountain is <u>covering</u> with snow. → _____

2 I was <u>interesting</u> in studying math. → _____

3 The lake is full of <u>swum</u> fish. → _____

4 Look at the sun <u>risen</u> above the horizon. → _____

5 This <u>sleep</u> princess is so beautiful. → _____

6 This <u>breaking</u> vase is my favorite. → _____

7 There are many <u>ran</u> people in the street. → _____

8 We have to respect all <u>live</u> things. → _____

9 The movie was very <u>excited</u>. → _____

10 She read a story <u>writing</u> in English. → _____

11 That <u>stealing</u> car was found there. → _____

12 People were <u>surprising</u> at the news. → _____

13 A ship is <u>floated</u> on the river. → _____

14 I felt something <u>moved</u> on my back. → _____

15 Do you know the man <u>talks</u> with Ann? → _____

16 The box <u>making</u> of wood is mine. → _____

다음 주어진 단어를 알맞은 형태로 바꾸어 빈칸에 쓰세요.

history 역사
football 풋볼
customer 소비자
trip 여행
decision 결정
marriage 결혼
death 죽음

1 (interest)   He heard some _____ news from me.

Amy is _____ in studying history.

2 (excite)   The football game was _____.

I was _____ at the football game.

3 (satisfy)   The customer was _____ at the service.

It is one of the most _____ jobs.

4 (surprise)   It was a _____ news.

He was not _____ at the news.

5 (tire)   I was really _____ after the trip.

The work was very _____.

6 (disappoint)   The dinner was _____.

She was _____ with his song.

7 (confuse)   We are _____ with his decision.

We are angry with his _____ decision.

8 (shock)   Her marriage is _____ news to us.

We were _____ by the news of his death.

다음 우리말과 같도록 주어진 단어를 배열하여 문장을 완성하세요.

onion 양파
bark 짖다
amazing 굉장한
park 주차하다

1 피아노를 치고 있는 남자는 누구니? (playing, the piano, man)

→ Who is the _____?

2 이것은 중고 컴퓨터이다. (used, is, a, computer)

→ This _____.

3 그녀는 구운 양파를 좋아한다. (onions, baked, likes)

→ She _____.

4 짖고 있는 저 개들을 무서워하지 마라. (dogs, barking, those)

→ Don't be afraid of _____.

5 그것은 정말 굉장한 이야기이구나! (story, an, it, amazing, is)

→ What _____!

6 문 옆에 주차된 자전거를 보아라. (bike, the door, parked, by)

→ Look at the _____.

7 소방관들은 불타고 있는 건물로 돌진했다. (burning, the, building)

→ The fire fighters rushed into _____.

8 Jill은 자신의 성적에 만족했다. (grade, with, satisfied, her)

→ Jill was _____.

9 벽에 걸린 그림을 보아라. (hung, picture, the wall, on)

→ Look at the _____.

10 너는 자고 있는 아기를 돌봐야만 한다. (sleeping, the, of, baby)

→ You should take care _____.

[1~2] 다음 중 문장의 빈칸에 알맞은 것을 고르세요.

1 The girl _____ a red hat is Jack's sister.
① wear　　　② wearing
③ wore　　　④ to wear

2 This is the _____ bicycle.
① steal　　　② stealing
③ stolen　　　④ to steal

[3~4] 다음 문장에서 어색한 부분을 찾아 바르게 고쳐 쓰세요.

3
I like the boy stood in front of the big tree.

_____ → _____

4
They found the bag throwing in the woods.

_____ → _____

[5~6] 다음 우리말과 같도록 빈칸에 들어갈 알맞은 것을 고르세요.

5
큰 소리로 이야기하고 있는 소년은 Bill이다.
→ The boy _____ loudly is Bill.

① talk　　　② to talk
③ talked　　　④ talking

6
나는 일본어로 쓰인 몇 권의 책을 가지고 있다.
→ I have some books _____ in Japanese.

① written　　　② write
③ to write　　　④ writing

7 다음 대화의 빈칸에 들어갈 말이 바르게 짝지어진 것을 고르세요.

A: Mark, Why are you _____?
B: I heard the news from Jill.
　　It's very _____.

① surprised − surprising
② surprised − surprised
③ surprising − surprised
④ surprising − surprising

8 다음 밑줄 친 부분의 쓰임이 〈보기〉와 같은 것을 고르세요.

〈보기〉 Do you know the <u>smiling</u> girl?

① His bobby is <u>collecting</u> coins.
② <u>Asking</u> for help is necessary.
③ My mom is <u>waiting</u> for me.
④ His job is <u>selling</u> cars.

9 다음 글의 밑줄 친 부분 중 어법상 어색한 것을 고르세요.

I liked ① <u>to see</u> the top of the mountain ② <u>covering</u> with snow. But it was ③ <u>disappointing</u>. We didn't have ④ <u>much</u> snow in winter.

10 다음 중 밑줄 친 부분의 쓰임이 <u>다른</u> 하나를 고르세요.

① <u>Driving</u> to Busan took 5 hours.
② She likes <u>wearing</u> earrings.
③ He is good at <u>cooking</u>.
④ Look at the <u>sleeping</u> baby.

[11~12] 다음 괄호 안에 알맞은 분사의 형태를 고르세요.

11 This machine isn't (worked / working).

12 The (injuring / injured) girl was taken to the hospital.

[13~14] 다음 주어진 단어를 우리말에 맞게 고쳐 쓰세요.

13 그녀는 지금 공원에서 산책하고 있다.
→ She is _____ a walk in the park now. (take)

14 나는 며칠 전에 잃어버린 그 반지를 찾았다.
→ I found the ring _____ a few days ago. (lose)

15 다음 빈칸에 들어갈 말로 알맞은 것을 고르세요.

I like the shirt _____ in the window

① display ② displaying
③ to display ④ displayed

16 다음 문장을 읽고, 현재분사와 과거분사를 이용해서 문장을 완성하세요.

The man frightened the girl.

→ The man was _____.
→ The girl was _____.

Step
5

A 우리말과 같도록 주어진 단어를 바르게 배열하여 완성하세요.

1 나는 구운 옥수수를 좋아한다. (baked, corns, like)

→ I _____.

2 그 어린이들은 달리는 버스에서 그에게 손을 흔들었다. (on, running, the bus)

→ The children waved to him _____.

3 그 나무 아래 누워 있는 남자는 Joe이다. (lying, under the tree, the man)

→ _____ is Joe.

B 다음 우리말을 참고하여 빈칸에 형용사로 쓰이는 분사를 쓰세요.

현재분사	과거분사
'~하게 하는'	'~하게 된'
confusing 당황하게 하는	_____ 당황한
_____ 걱정스러운	worried 걱정되는
_____ 놀라운	_____ 놀란
_____ 지루한	_____ 지루해진
_____ 흥분시키는	_____ 흥분한
_____ 충격적인	_____ 충격 받은
_____ 재미있는	_____ 재미를 느끼는

문장의 형식 1

문장의 주요소와 수식요소를 구분할 수 있다.

문장의 구성요소에 따른 5개 문장 형식을 구분할 수 있다.

문장의 주요소는 문장을 구성하는 데 반드시 있어야 하는 요소로 주어, 동사, 목적어, 보어가 있어요. 수식요소는 주어, 동사, 목적어, 보어를 뺀 나머지이며 주요소를 꾸며 주는 역할을 해요. 또한 문장에서 주요소의 구성에 따라 1~5형식으로 문장을 구분해요.

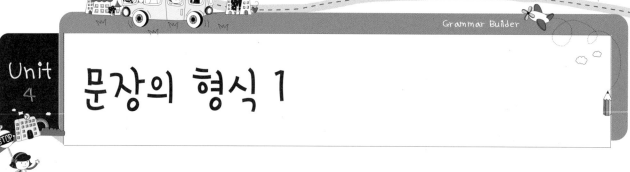

Unit 4

문장의 형식 1

1. 문장의 주요소와 수식요소

문장의 주요소는 문장을 구성하는 데 반드시 있어야 하는 요소로 주어, 동사, 목적어, 보어가 있다.

- 주요소: 주어(Subject), 동사(Verb), 목적어(Object), 보어(Complement)
- 수식요소: 부사, 부사구, 전치사구 → 수식어구(Modifier)

We live. 우리는 산다.
S   V

We live near the church. 우리는 교회 근처에 산다.
S   V   M

> 문장의 형식을
> 1~5형식으로 나눌 때는
> 주요소만으로 구분한다.

2. 1형식 문장

〈주어＋동사〉로 이루어진 문장으로 부사(구)나 전치사구가 오기도 하지만 이들은 수식어로 문장의 형식을 결정하는데 역할을 하지 않는다.

A bird sings. 새가 노래한다.
  S   V

A bird sings in the morning. 새가 아침에 노래한다.
  S   V   M

A bird sings in the tree in the morning. 새가 나무에서 아침에 노래한다.
  S   V   M   M

3. 2형식 문장

〈주어＋동사＋보어〉로 이루어진 문장으로 보어 자리에는 명사 또는 형용사가 와서 주어를 보충 설명해 준다.

• 감각을 나타내는 동사(look, sound, smell, taste, fell)는 보어가 부사처럼 해석될 때도 있지만 형용사가 온다. ▶ Unit 5에서 학습

He is a police officer. 그는 경찰관이다.
S V   C

The baby was sick last night. 그 아기는 어제 밤에 아팠다.
  S   V   C   M

Cathy looks beautiful. Cathy는 아름답게 보인다.
  S   V   C

> **Pop Quiz**　I. 다음 문장에서 주어에는 S, 동사에는 V를 쓰세요.
> ❶ The frog jumps high.　　❷ My father is a scientist.

4. 3형식 문장

〈주어＋동사＋목적어〉로 이루어진 문장으로 목적어는 '~을/를'로 해석하며 목적어 자리에는 명사 또는 대명사가 온다.

Thomas likes apples. Thomas는 사과를 좋아한다.
  S   V   O

We bought a computer. 우리는 컴퓨터를 샀다.
S   V   O

She loves him very much. 그녀는 그를 매우 많이 사랑한다.
 S   V   O   M

5. 4형식 문장

〈주어＋동사＋간접목적어(~에게)＋직접목적어(…을/를)〉로 이루어진 문장으로 간접목적어(IO)에는 사람이, 직접목적어(DO)에는 사물이 온다.

• 목적어를 2개 취하는 동사를 수여동사(give, make, buy, send, tell, hand, show, teach 등)라고 한다. ▶ Unit 5에서 학습

She teaches them English. 그녀는 그들에게 영어를 가르친다.
　S　　V　　IO　　DO

His father gave him a ball. 그의 아버지는 그에게 공을 주었다.
　　S　　　V　　IO　DO

6. 5형식 문장

〈주어＋동사＋목적어＋목적격 보어〉로 이루어진 문장으로 목적격 보어 자리에는 명사 또는 형용사가 와서 목적어를 보충 설명해 준다.

• 동사 want, ask, tell, advise 등은 목적격 보어로 to부정사를 쓴다. ▶ Unit 5에서 학습

She makes us happy. 그녀는 우리를 행복하게 한다.
　S　　V　　O　　C

He called the dog "Smile." 그는 그 개를 Smile이라고 불렀다.
　S　　V　　O　　　C

They wanted me to study hard. 그들은 내가 열심히 공부하기를 원했다.
　S　　V　　O　　　C

Pop Quiz　2. 다음 문장이 몇 형식인지 숫자로 쓰세요.

❶ We buy a new computer. (　　)

❷ He made her sad. (　　)

다음에서 주어와 동사에 밑줄을 긋고, S(주어)와 V(동사)를 쓰세요.

rise 떠오르다
behavior 행동
greedy 욕심 많은
soldier 군인

1   We met him yesterday.

2   The sun rises in the east.

3   Jack and you are very handsome.

4   My friend sent me an e-mail then.

5   His behavior made us angry.

6   He and she are kind to everyone.

7   They are in the classroom now.

8   The leaves become red and yellow.

9   John played tennis with his friend.

10 My teacher asked me a question.

11 The greedy man smiles in his house.

12 The soldiers dig many holes.

13 The young woman gave him candies.

14 A big bird flew in the sky yesterday.

다음에서 보어나 목적어에 밑줄을 긋고, C(보어) 또는 O(목적어)를 쓰세요.

leader 지도자
vegetable 야채
island 섬
sour 신

1 Peter became the leader.

2 The students will be good men.

3 The old man buys the vegetables.

4 My dog is white and big.

5 They watched TV all day yesterday.

6 John and his brother are reading books.

7 The bread smells good.

8 He drew the pictures on the island.

9 The boys look sleepy.

10 The woman was sick last week.

11 She loves Brian very much.

12 The old woman opens the window.

13 The oranges taste sour.

14 My mother bought a nice dress.

다음에서 동사와 목적격 보어에 밑줄을 긋고, V(동사)와 C(목적격 보어)를 쓰세요.

1 His father made him a movie star.

2 They painted the wall green.

3 Every teacher thinks Cathy smart.

4 She always makes me comfortable.

5 We called the black cat "Pluto."

6 Food and trash can make water dirty.

7 The students found the quiz difficult.

8 The wave made my clothes wet.

9 I think the movie touching.

10 The baker made the cake beautiful.

11 They call him a walking dictionary.

12 I found the book interesting.

13 John and Ann named their baby Tony.

14 The doctor advised me to exercise.

comfortable 편안한
trash 쓰레기
quiz 퀴즈
wave 파도
touching 감동적인
advise 충고하다

다음 주어진 단어들을 바르게 배열하여 문장을 완성하세요.

useful 유용한
empty 비어 있는, 빈
lift 승강기
treasure 보물

1 me / my brother / made / angry

→ _____

2 a question / us / asked / the teacher

→ _____

3 they / useful information / me / give

→ _____

4 found / empty / Judy and Kate / the box

→ _____

5 bought / the man / her / the flowers

→ _____

6 wrote / her parents / Sally / a letter

→ _____

7 English people / call / lifts / elevators

→ _____

8 the prince / the treasure / them / gave

→ _____

9 the earth / clean / should keep / we

→ _____

10 Brian / a lot of e-mails / sent / me

→ _____

다음 문장에서 밑줄 친 부분의 문장 성분을 쓰세요.

1 He is reading <u>the magazine</u>. → _____

2 The kind girl shows <u>him</u> the way. → _____

3 The rabbits <u>run</u> fast. → _____

4 My parents want me <u>to study hard</u>. → _____

5 That sounds <u>interesting</u>. → _____

6 I think the movie <u>funny</u>. → _____

7 He <u>doesn't eat</u> fast food. → _____

8 <u>Lisa and Billy</u> like classical music. → _____

9 My mom asked me a <u>question</u>. → _____

10 Mr. Smith teaches <u>us</u> science. → _____

11 The cake tastes <u>sweet</u>. → _____

12 She gave <u>her friend</u> the card. → _____

13 <u>I</u> went there with my mother. → _____

14 <u>He and she</u> danced on the stage. → _____

15 Her voice is very <u>beautiful</u>. → _____

16 My father builds the <u>nice</u> house. → _____

way 길
rabbit 토끼
stage 무대
voice 목소리
build 짓다

문장의 형식 1 · **83**

다음 문장이 몇 형식인지 괄호 안에 숫자로 쓰세요.

scientist 과학자
living room 거실
brave 용감한
thick 두꺼운

1 A bird sings under the tree.   (   )

2 She always makes me happy.   (   )

3 He became a great scientist.   (   )

4 Ann and Lucy are making cards.   (   )

5 My father named me Jennifer.   (   )

6 It gives them useful information.   (   )

7 She watches TV in the living room.   (   )

8 The dog runs fast in the park.   (   )

9 They called their dog Derby.   (   )

10 Jenny plays tennis every day.   (   )

11 He is a brave fire fighter.   (   )

12 Two women live in the little town.   (   )

13 The boy gave him a ball.   (   )

14 This is an old table.   (   )

15 He is digging a hole on the hill.   (   )

16 Tom found the book thick.   (   )

Build Up 3

다음 문장이 몇 형식인지 괄호 안에 숫자로 쓰세요.

1 We play baseball every Sunday. (   )

2 The students studied hard. (   )

3 They call the cat Happy. (   )

4 Sarah bought him a nice shirt. (   )

5 She gets up early in the morning. (   )

6 They thought Tom kind. (   )

7 Jane and Eric are very upset. (   )

8 Brian gave me some candies. (   )

9 The butterflies fly high in the sky. (   )

10 He became a famous painter. (   )

11 We will often visit you. (   )

12 She made her son a pair of mittens. (   )

13 The cookies smell very sweet. (   )

14 He and she are talking about something. (   )

15 She advised me to eat more vegetables. (   )

16 The accident happened suddenly. (   )

upset 화가 난
rice 쌀
painter 화가
mitten 벙어리장갑
accident 사고

다음 빈칸에 알맞은 말을 쓰세요.

I 문장의 주요소는 문장을 구성하는 데 반드시 있어야 하는 요소로 _____, _____, _____, _____ 가 있다.

• 수식요소: 부사, 부사구, 전치사구 → _____ 구(Modifier)

2 1형식 문장은 〈_____ + _____〉로 이루어진 문장으로 부사(구)나 전치사구가 오기도 하지만 이들은 수식어로 문장의 형식을 결정하는데 역할을 하지 않는다.

3 2형식 문장은 〈_____ + _____ + _____〉로 이루어진 문장으로 보어 자리에는 명사 또는 _____ 가 와서 주어를 보충 설명해 준다.

• 감각을 나타내는 동사(look, sound, smell, taste, fell)는 보어가 부사처럼 해석될 때도 있지만 _____ 가 온다.

4 3형식 문장은 〈_____ + _____ + _____〉로 이루어진 문장으로 목적어는 '∼을/를'로 해석하며 목적어 자리에는 _____ 또는 대명사가 온다.

5 4형식 문장은 〈주어+동사+ _____ (∼에게)+ _____ (∼을/를)〉로 이루어진 문장으로 간접목적어에는 _____ 이, 직접목적어에는 _____ 이 온다.

• 목적어를 2개 취하는 동사를 _____ 동사(give, make, buy, send, tell, hand, teach, show 등)라고 한다.

6 5형식 문장은 〈주어+동사+ _____ + _____〉로 이루어진 문장으로 목적격 보어 자리에는 명사 또는 _____ 가 와서 목적어를 보충 설명해 준다.

• 동사 want, ask, tell, advise 등은 목적격 보어로 _____ 를 쓴다.

다음 문장이 몇 형식인지 괄호 안에 숫자로 쓰고, 밑줄 친 부분의
문장 성분도 쓰세요. (주어-S, 동사-V, 목적어-O, 보어-C)

cave 동굴
strange 이상한
iced (얼음으로) 차게 한
bake 굽다

1   The bear sleeps in this cave.   (   )

2   His mother made him a doctor.   (   )

3   Kevin wrote a letter yesterday.   (   )

4   His story sounds strange.   (   )

5   The children play on the playground.   (   )

6   Peter bought his son a toy.   (   )

7   Everyone thinks Linda smart.   (   )

8   This iced coffee tastes good.   (   )

9   I gave my girlfriend a gift.   (   )

10 We think him a police officer.   (   )

11 My mother baked some cookies.   (   )

12 They went to the zoo by subway.   (   )

다음 문장이 몇 형식인지 괄호 안에 숫자로 쓰고, 밑줄 친 부분의 문장 성분도 쓰세요. (주어-S, 동사-V, 목적어-O, 보어-C)

terrible 지독한, 무서운
test 시험
lend 빌려주다
dead 죽은
thirsty 목마른

1 The room smelled very terrible. ( )

2 She showed him her pictures. ( )

3 Harry bought an expensive computer. ( )

4 He found the test difficult. ( )

5 We saw the movie last Sunday. ( )

6 My backpack is in my room. ( )

7 The bank opens at nine o'clock. ( )

8 The boy finished his homework yesterday. ( )

9 She lends me some money. ( )

10 They found their dog dead. ( )

11 He looks thirsty and hungry. ( )

12 The girl speaks English very well. ( )

다음 문장이 몇 형식인지 괄호 안에 숫자로 쓰고, 밑줄 친 부분의
문장 성분도 쓰세요. (주어-S, 동사-V, 목적어-O, 보어-C)

soft 부드러운
genius 천재
lawyer 변호사
reporter 기자
kindness 친절

1 Bill teaches his students math. (   )

2 Mary likes a big teddy bear. (   )

3 They stayed in London for a week. (   )

4 Linda plays the guitar on Wednesdays. (   )

5 This scarf feels soft. (   )

6 People call the kid a genius. (   )

7 The summer vacation begins in July. (   )

8 He became a wise lawyer. (   )

9 The reporter asked the actor questions. (   )

10 The children are swimming in the lake. (   )

11 His kindness made her happy. (   )

12 We brushed our teeth after dinner. (   )

[1~4] 다음 문장의 밑줄 친 부분에 해당하는 것을 〈보기〉에서 골라 쓰세요.

〈보기〉	주격 보어	목적어
	직접목적어	목적격 보어

1 She is a <u>famous singer</u>.

→ _____

2 I will send her <u>the photos</u>.

→ _____

3 Her smile makes me <u>happy</u>.

→ _____

4 Mr. Smith bought <u>the bike</u>.

→ _____

5 다음 문장의 밑줄 친 부분 중 목적어인 것을 고르세요.

① <u>Lucy</u> will ② <u>buy</u> ③ <u>her sweater</u> at the department store ④ <u>tomorrow</u>.

6 다음 중 밑줄 친 부분의 역할이 <u>잘못</u> 연결된 것을 고르세요.

① His wife is <u>wise</u>. (목적격 보어)

② The girls <u>like</u> music. (동사)

③ He taught <u>us</u> math. (간접목적어)

④ I found <u>the box</u> full. (목적어)

[7~8] 다음 문장과 문장의 형식이 같은 문장을 고르세요.

7 Brian feels sleepy.

① Andy likes his parents.

② She gave me some money.

③ He plays on the playground.

④ They are close friends.

8 Joe lives in the small town.

① They call him "Prince."

② My brother swims very well.

③ I know the funny movie.

④ Jack showed Jenny the book.

9 다음 중 문장의 형식이 나머지 셋과 다른 것을 고르세요.

① Judy have many flowers.
② Matt drives the new car.
③ Billy walks to the library.
④ I don't want to meet the girl.

10 다음 중 문장의 빈칸에 알맞은 것을 고르세요.

> My mother will tell _____.

① a story me
② a story I
③ me a story
④ I a story

[11~12] 다음 괄호 안에서 알맞은 단어를 고르세요.

11 The food smells (bad / badly).

12 They look (serious / seriously).

13 The soup smells (good / well).

[14~15] 다음 문장이 몇 형식인지 쓰세요.

14 My sister gave your message to her.
( )

15 My grandmother showed him many toys. ( )

[16~17] 다음 괄호 안에서 알맞은 것을 고르세요.

16 They found our dog (dead / to dead).

17 Please call (I / me) James.

[18~20] 다음 괄호 안의 동사를 알맞은 형태로 바꿔 써 보세요.

18 I want them _____ (come) on time.

19 My mother advised me _____ (exercise) every day.

20 The students found the quiz _____. (easy)

A 다음 우리말과 같도록 괄호 안의 말을 바르게 배열하세요.

1 Jenny가 Tom에게 선물을 주었다. (Jenny, the gift, gave, Tom)

→ _____

2 우리는 아기를 Dan이라고 이름 지었다. (Dan, the baby, we, named)

→ _____

3 Sam은 그 나무 뒤에 서 있다. (behind, is standing, Sam, the tree)

→ _____

B 다음 밑줄 친 문장이 몇 형식인지 쓰세요.

1. Helen works at school. 2. She teaches them science. 3. She is a good
teacher. 4. All the students like her. 5. They call her "Woman Einstein."

1 _____ **2** _____

3 _____ **4** _____

5 _____

Unit 5

문장의 형식 2

감각동사+형용사의 쓰임을 이해하고 활용할 수 있다.

수여동사의 의미와 쓰임을 이해하고 활용할 수 있다.

5형식 문장의 다양한 쓰임을 이해할 수 있다.

2형식 문장에서 감각을 나타내는 동사 뒤에 오는 보어가 부사처럼 해석되지만 이들 동사 뒤에는 형용사가 와요. 4형식 문장의 동사를 수여동사라고 하는데, '주다'의 의미가 포함되어 있어서 수여동사라고 불려요. 또한 5형식 문장에서 목적격 보어에는 명사, 형용사, to부정사 등 다양한 형태가 올 수 있어요.

Unit 5

문장의 형식 2

1. 2형식 문장 - 감각동사

감각을 나타내내는 동사에는 look, sound, smell, taste, feel 등이 있다.

• 감각동사 뒤에 보어는 부사처럼 해석되지만 형용사가 온다.

look(~하게 보이다)		Your father looks busy. busily (×)
sound(~하게 들리다)		His story sounds strange.
feel(~하게 느껴지다)	+형용사	The scarf feels soft.
smell(~한 냄새가 나다)		The soup smells delicious.
taste(~한 맛이 나다)		Honey tastes sweet.

Cathy looks like a model.
Cathy는 모델처럼 보인다.

감각동사 뒤에 like가 오면 뒤에 명사를 쓰고
'~처럼 ~하다'로 해석한다.

Pop Quiz　Ⅰ. 다음 괄호 안에서 알맞은 것을 고르세요.
❶ It tastes (sweetly, sweet).　　❷ You look (happy, happily).

2. 4형식 문장 - 수여동사

'~에게 …을 (해)주다'라는 뜻이 포함되어 있어서 수여동사라고 부른다.

• 수여동사: give, send, show, teach, tell, buy, make, cook, ask, sing 등

- 의미: ~에게 …을 (해)주다

  Kevin gave me a letter. Kevin은 나에게 편지를 주었다.

  She bought her son a toy. 그녀는 그녀의 아들에게 장난감을 사 주었다.

  He explained the rules to us. 그는 우리에게 규칙을 설명했다. (수여동사 ×)

수여동사로 착각하기
쉬운 동사:
explain, suggest,
introduce

3. 4형식 문장의 3형식 전환

4형식 문장은 간접목적어와 직접목적어의 순서를 바꾸고 간접목적어 앞에 전치사를 써서 3형식 문장으로 바꿀 수 있다.

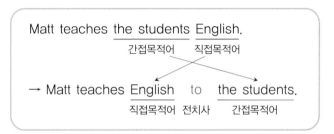

4형식을 3형식으로
전환할 때 필요한 전치사

to를 쓰는 동사	give, send, bring, teach, show, tell, write, pass, lend 등
for를 쓰는 동사	make, buy, cook, sing, get 등
of를 쓰는 동사	ask

She made them a cheese cake. (4형식) → She made a cheese cake for them. (3형식)

그녀는 그들에게 치즈 케이크를 만들어 주었다.

Jane asked me some questions. (4형식) → Jane asked some questions of me. (3형식)

Jane은 나에게 약간의 질문을 했다.

Pop Quiz **2.** 다음 괄호 안에서 알맞은 것을 고르세요.

❶ He buys flowers (to, for) her. ❷ She sent an e-mail (to, of) me.

4. 5형식 문장 - 목적격 보어

5형식 문장의 목적격 보어에는 명사, 형용사, to부정사 등이 올 수 있다.

(1) 목적격 보어가 명사인 경우: 목적어의 동일 대상

call(~을 …라고 부르다), name(~을 …라고 이름 짓다), make(~을 …로 만들다), choose(~을 …로 뽑다)	+목적어+목적격 보어 (명사)

They named the baby Ann. 그들은 그 아기를 Ann이라고 이름지었다.

(2) 목적격 보어가 형용사인 경우: 목적어의 성질이나 상태

make(~을 …하게 만들다), keep(~을 …하게 유지하다), find(~이 …하는 것을 알게 되다)	+목적어+목적격 보어 (형용사)

The new made them happy. 그 소식은 그들을 행복하게 만들었다.

(3) 목적격 보어가 to부정사인 경우: 목적어의 동작이나 행동

want(~가 …하기를 원하다), tell(~에게 …하라고 말하다), ask(~에게 …해 달라고 부탁하다), expect(~가 …하기를 기대하다), allow(~가 …하는 것을 허락하다), advise(~에게 …하도록 조언하다)	+목적어+목적격 보어 (to부정사)

I want you to come to the party. 나는 네가 그 파티에 오기를 원한다.

Pop Quiz

3. 다음 괄호 안에서 알맞은 것을 고르세요.

❶ I found the book (sad, sadly).

❷ She asked me (visit, to visit) him sometime.

다음 괄호 안에서 알맞은 것을 골라 동그라미 하세요.

smooth 부드러운
bitter 쓴
rough 거친
serious 진지한

1 The room smelled very (terrible, terribly).

2 The lemons taste (sour, sourly).

3 The flowers look (beautiful, beautifully).

4 The clothes feel (smooth, smoothly).

5 This bell sounds (sweet, sweetly).

6 That sofa looks (comfortable, comfortably).

7 The man looks (like, ×) a monkey.

8 The medicine tastes (bitter, bitterly).

9 The bread smells (bad, badly).

10 He looks (wise, wisely) and (clever, cleverly).

11 This paper feels (rough, roughly).

12 The old man looks (strong, strongly).

13 Her story sounds (strangely, strange).

14 This soap smells (good, well).

15 You look (serious, seriously) today.

16 This puzzle looks (difficult, difficultly).

다음 괄호 안에서 알맞은 것을 골라 동그라미 하세요.

fairy tale 동화
album 앨범
postcard 엽서

1 Mr. Brown teaches (us math, math us).

2 Sue made sandwiches (for, of) the kids.

3 She lends an eraser (for, to) him.

4 She asked their names (to, of) the students.

5 We showed (our pictures her, her our pictures).

6 Please pass the sugar (to, of) me.

7 Sally asked (him his address, his address him).

8 My uncle told (fairy tales her, her fairy tales).

9 My brother wrote an e-mail (to, for) his friend.

10 He made a nice chair (to, for) his daughter.

11 Jane gave (candies him, him candies).

12 Tom and Sam showed the album (to, for) me.

13 She sent (me a postcard, a postcard me).

14 David gave some roses (to, for) Cathy.

15 Mom made (us some cookies, some cookies us).

16 I will buy (my son a desk, a desk my son).

다음 괄호 안에서 알맞은 것을 골라 동그라미 하세요.

message 메시지
baker 제빵사
map 지도

1 My mother bought an umbrella (for, to) me.

2 My brother gave your message (to, for) her.

3 He told many interesting stories (to, of) us.

4 She wrote an e-mail (to, for) her teacher.

5 My sister lends some money (to, of) me.

6 The man made a big kite (to, for) his son.

7 They buy (me, for me) a new computer.

8 She sent a letter (to her father, her father).

9 Brandon teaches math (to them, them).

10 The man got some flowers (her, for her).

11 The teacher asks (me, of me) an easy question.

12 Jane cooked a cake (her friend, for her friend).

13 Brian gave (Susan, to Susan) a ring.

14 The baker made cookies (his son, for his son).

15 We asked many question (to him, of him).

16 John gave (his brother, to his brother) a map.

다음 괄호 안에서 알맞은 것을 골라 동그라미 하세요.

club 클럽

star 인기 배우

1 She asked him (to go, go) to bed.

2 His mother made (for him, him) a doctor.

3 We thought Julia (smartly, smart).

4 He allowed me (to take, take) a walk.

5 He advised me (exercise, to exercise) regularly.

6 She named the cat (Butterfly, to Butterfly).

7 My brother made me (happy, happily).

8 He found the test (difficult, difficulty).

9 I advise him (read, to read) the book.

10 Tom told us (to join, join) the club.

11 I allow her (to spend, spend) some money.

12 The movie made her (a star, to a star).

13 My dad told (me, to me) to study hard.

14 My mother calls me (Prince, to Prince).

15 She allowed us (to play, playing) with dolls.

16 He asked me (to call, call) him after school.

다음 우리말과 같도록 동사를 골라 주어진 단어를 사용하여 완성하세요.

cloth 천

handsome 잘생긴

look   smell   sound   feel   taste

1 그 수프는 맛있는 냄새가 난다. (delicious)

= The soup _____ _____ .

2 우리 선생님은 정말 화가 나 보였다. (angry)

= Our teacher _____ really _____ .

3 이 냉커피는 단 맛이 난다. (sweet)

= This iced coffee _____ _____ .

4 그녀의 목소리는 아름답게 들린다. (beautiful)

= Her voice _____ _____ .

5 그 바지는 너한테 너무 짧아 보인다. (short)

= Those pants _____ too _____ for you.

6 이 천은 부드러운 느낌이 난다. (soft)

= This cloth _____ _____ .

7 이 초콜릿은 쓴 맛이 난다. (bitter)

= This chocolate _____ _____ .

8 그 빵은 좋은 냄새가 난다. (good)

= The bread _____ _____ .

9 Jonathan은 오늘 잘생겨 보인다. (handsome)

= Jonathan _____ _____ today.

다음 빈칸에 주어진 말을 알맞은 형태로 바꾸어 쓰세요.

cheer 격려하다
hamster 햄스터
marry 결혼하다
pencil case 필통

1 She asked me _____ pictures. (take)

2 These candies tastes _____. (delicious)

3 I wanted you _____ home early. (come)

4 This water feels very _____. (cold)

5 They told the girl _____ up. (cheer)

6 Dan asked a lot of questions _____. (her)

7 His voice sounds _____. (strange)

8 My uncle made a toy car _____. (me)

9 They allow him _____ to the party. (go)

10 Your hamsters look _____. (cute)

11 He wrote a letter _____. (his teacher)

12 Lucy showed her pictures _____. (them)

13 Her father allowed her _____ him. (marry)

14 He asked me _____ him with his work. (help)

15 Please pass that pencil case _____. (John)

16 I advise her _____ every day. (exercise)

다음 주어진 말과 감각동사를 사용하여 문장을 완성하세요.

scarf 스카프
lemon 레몬

1 This shirt _____ _____ for him. (short)

이 셔츠는 그에게 작아 보인다.

2 His voice _____ _____. (good)

그의 목소리는 좋게 들렸다.

3 The scarf _____ very _____. (smooth)

그 스카프는 매우 부드럽게 느껴진다.

4 This lemon _____ _____. (sour)

이 레몬은 신 맛이 난다.

5 The coffee _____ _____. (sweet)

그 커피는 달콤한 냄새가 난다.

다음 문장의 빈칸에 알맞은 전치사를 쓰세요.

6 Mary gave some carrots _____ the horse.

7 She asked an easy question _____ the kid.

8 My aunt made sandwiches _____ us.

9 Peter brought my bike _____ me.

10 We bought some flowers _____ Sally.

11 He sent an e-mail _____ Matt last night.

12 Brian told the happy news _____ them.

 Build Up 2

다음 4형식 문장을 3형식 문장으로 고쳐 쓰세요.

cousin 사촌

artist 화가

1 David gave him a birthday present.

→ _____

2 We made Lisa a big chocolate cake.

→ _____

3 Daniel bought his mom a yellow scarf.

→ _____

4 My sister asked me a strange question.

→ _____

5 Peter buys his cousin an interesting book.

→ _____

6 Mr. Johnson taught them history.

→ _____

7 My aunt cooked her daughter spaghetti.

→ _____

8 Tony wrote his friend an e-mail.

→ _____

9 He always asks us difficult questions.

→ _____

10 The artist showed her some pictures.

→ _____

다음 3형식 문장을 4형식으로, 4형식 문장을 3형식으로 고쳐 쓰세요.

rose 장미
diamond 다이아몬드
snack 간식
secretary 비서

1 His father bought her a pink dress.

→ _____

2 Tom made nice kites for the children.

→ _____

3 Andy gave me a lot of roses.

→ _____

4 My grandfather told us many stories.

→ _____

5 The girl asked some questions of me.

→ _____

6 The man gave a diamond ring to her.

→ _____

7 My uncle sent me a Christmas present.

→ _____

8 The teacher bought some snacks for them.

→ _____

9 The secretary handed the book to him.

→ _____

10 Dave lent my brother his bicycle.

→ _____

다음 빈칸에 알맞은 말을 쓰세요.

1 감각동사에는 look(~하게 보이다), _____(~하게 들리다), _____(~한 냄새가 나다), _____(~한 맛이 나다), feel(~하게 느껴지다) 등이 있는데, 감각동사 뒤에 보어는 부사처럼 해석되지만 _____가 온다.

2 감각동사 뒤에 _____가 오면 뒤에 명사를 쓰고 '~처럼 …하다'로 해석한다.

3 '~에게 …을 (해)주다'라는 뜻이 포함되어 있는 동사를 _____라고 부르며, 동사에는 give, send, show, teach, tell, buy, make, cook, sing, ask 등이다.

4 4형식 문장을 간접목적어와 직접목적어의 순서를 바꾸고 _____ 앞에 전치사를 써서 _____ 형식 문장으로 바꿀 수 있다.

Matt teaches the students English. (4형식)

→ Matt teaches _____. (3형식)

전치사 _____를 쓰는 동사	give, send, bring, teach, show, write, tell, pass, lend 등
전치사 _____를 쓰는 동사	make, buy, cook, sing, get 등
전치사 of를 쓰는 동사	_____

5 5형식 문장의 목적격 보어에는 명사, 형용사, to부정사 등이 올 수 있다.

• 목적격 보어가 _____인 경우는 목적어의 동일 대상을 나타낸다.

• 목적격 보어가 _____인 경우는 목적어의 성질이나 상태를 나타낸다.

• 목적격 보어가 _____인 경우는 목적어의 동작이나 행동을 나타낸다.

다음 문장에서 밑줄 친 부분을 바르게 고쳐 쓰세요.

scary 무서운

complete 완성하다

1 My father asked some questions <u>to me</u>. → _____

2 He advised me <u>exercise</u> every day. → _____

3 This melon tastes <u>sweetly</u>. → _____

4 Mrs. White teaches science <u>for us</u>. → _____

5 The movie made the students <u>sadly</u>. → _____

6 She allowed me <u>going</u> to the party. → _____

7 Please tell a scary story <u>us</u>. → _____

8 Her uncle looked very <u>busily</u>. → _____

9 My brother sent her <u>to the box</u>. → _____

10 They asked me <u>of take</u> pictures. → _____

11 These cookies smell <u>well</u>. → _____

12 My mom bought a nice bike <u>to me</u>. → _____

13 He wants you <u>complete</u> the work. → _____

14 Jordan taught them <u>for basketball</u>. → _____

15 Cathy looks <u>likes</u> a model. → _____

16 He made a big bench <u>to his sons</u>. → _____

다음 우리말과 같도록 주어진 단어를 사용하여 문장을 완성하세요.

death 죽음

snowman 눈사람

1 그는 그녀가 파티에 오기를 원한다. (to, the party, to come)

→ He wants her _____.

2 Tom은 그녀에게 긴 편지를 쓴다. (a long letter, write, her)

→ Tom _____.

3 이 약은 쓴 맛이 난다. (bitter, taste)

→ This medicine _____.

4 그는 우리에게 그의 앨범을 보여 주었다. (showed, his album, us, to)

→ He _____.

5 그녀의 남편의 죽음은 그녀를 슬프게 만들었다. (her, made, sad)

→ The death of her husband _____.

6 이 음악은 이상하게 들린다. (sound, strange)

→ This music _____.

7 그는 나에게 눈사람을 만들어 주었다. (a snowman, me, for, made)

→ He _____.

8 나에게 설탕을 건네주세요. (the sugar, pass, me)

→ Please _____.

9 너는 오늘 행복해 보인다. (today, happy, look)

→ You _____.

10 그는 나에게 그녀의 이름을 물었다. (ask, of, her name, me)

→ He _____.

11 그들은 그 아기를 Cathy라고 불렀다. (Cathy, called, the baby)

→ They _____.

다음 괄호 안의 동사를 이용하여 문장을 바꿔 쓰세요.

foreigner 외국인

learn 배우다

1 Sally and Ann are beautiful. (look)

→ _____

2 The chicken soup is delicious. (smell)

→ _____

3 The silk is smooth and soft. (feel)

→ _____

4 His voice is tired. (sound)

→ _____

5 Chocolate is sweet and bitter. (taste)

→ _____

다음 괄호 안의 말을 바르게 배열하여 문장을 완성하세요.

6 (angry, my brother, made, me)

→ _____

7 (some questions, asked, the foreigner, us)

→ _____

8 (Mark, him, made, for, a model car)

→ _____

9 (the box, found, empty, my mother)

→ _____

10 (I wanted, to, learn, him, English)

→ _____

[1~2] 다음 중 빈칸에 알맞은 것을 고르세요.

1 My mother _____ a cake for me.

① made   ② gave

③ passed   ④ sent

2 My sister asked a strange question _____ me.

① to   ② of

③ for   ④ with

3 다음 대화의 밑줄 친 부분 중 어색한 것을 고르세요.

A: Cathy, you ① look happy today.

B: I ② feel good. Today is my birthday. ③ Can you come to my birthday party?

A: That ④ sounds greatly.

B: See you later.

[4~5] 다음 중 빈칸에 알맞지 않은 것을 고르세요.

4 The cookies taste _____.

① good   ② sweet

③ badly   ④ terrible

5 My father told me _____.

① to study hard

② to go to bed

③ to get up early

④ do my homework

6 다음 문장에서 밑줄 친 부분의 역할이 다른 것을 고르세요.

① He gave her <u>some flowers</u>.

② He wants her <u>to join the club</u>.

③ His mom made him <u>a doctor</u>.

④ They called her <u>Cinderella</u>.

[7~8] 다음 빈칸에 들어갈 말이 바르게 짝지어진 것을 고르세요.

7

> She bought a nice bike _____ him.
> Please show a letter _____ me.

① for – of   ② for – to

③ to – for   ④ of – for

8

> He teaches math _____ us.
> Mom allows me _____ play outside.

① to – for   ② for – for

③ for – to   ④ to – to

[9~10] 다음 밑줄 친 부분 중 어색한 것을 고르세요.

9 ① <u>John</u> ② <u>brought</u> ③ <u>to me</u> ④ <u>my kite</u>.

10 ① <u>The doctor</u> ② <u>advised</u> ③ <u>me</u> ④ <u>gets up early</u>.

11 다음 중 빈칸에 들어갈 말이 다른 것을 고르세요.

① She told a story _____ them.

② Please cook spaghetti _____ us.

③ Pass the salt _____ me.

④ He showed the album _____ her.

12 다음 중 밑줄 친 동사의 성격이 다른 것을 고르세요.

① He buys me a toy car.

② Sally wrote him a postcard.

③ Tell me your address, please.

④ He painted his door green.

13 다음 중 문장의 형식이 다른 것을 고르세요.

① He found the bottle empty.

② I will tell you big news.

③ We call him Black Joe.

④ He told me to cheer up.

[14~16] 다음 중 잘못된 문장을 고르세요.

14 ① She felt tired.

② Your shirt looks tight.

③ His voice sounds sweet.

④ The soup smells greatly.

15 ① I gave her some books.

② My uncle made kites me.

③ She showed him the pictures.

④ Please pass the ball to Eric.

16 ① The paper feels rough.

② Julia teaches English us.

③ Andy thought her a singer.

④ I want you to paint the wall.

[17~18] 다음 문장이 같도록 빈칸에 알맞은 말을 쓰세요.

17

> Harry sent me an e-mail yesterday.
> = Harry sent an e-mail _____ me yesterday.

→ _____

18

> I read the book. It was very funny.
> = I found the book very _____.

→ _____

[19~20] 다음 괄호 안의 문장을 이용하여 우리말을 영어로 쓰세요.

19 그것은 이상하게 들린다. (It is strange.)

→ _____

20 그 천은 부드럽게 느껴진다.
(The cloth is smooth.)

→ _____

A 다음 우리말과 같도록 빈칸에 알맞은 말을 쓰세요.

1 그녀의 노래는 아름답게 들린다.

→ Her song _____ _____.

2 이 방의 공기는 더럽게 느껴진다.

→ The air in this room _____ _____.

B 다음 그림을 보고, 〈보기〉의 표현을 이용하여 문장을 완성하세요.

Tom   Judy   Sally

| 〈보기〉 | a nice hat | an MP3 player |
| | a teddy bear | many books |

1 Tom gave _____ Sally.

2 Judy bought _____ Sally.

C 다음 표를 보고, Mark에게 바라는 것에 대한 문장을 완성하세요.

Mark's parents	eat more vegetables for his health
Mark's sister	help her with her homework
Mark's brother	spend more time with him

1 Mark's parents want him _____.

2 Mark's sister _____.

3 Mark's brother _____.

Unit
6

현재완료

현재완료의 의미와 형태를 이해하고 알 수 있다.

현재완료의 네 가지 쓰임을 이해하고 활용할 수 있다.

과거시제와 현재완료 문장을 구분할 수 있다.

과거의 어느 시점에 일어난 일이 지금까지 영향을 줄 때 현재완료를 사용하여 나타내요.

현재완료는 'have+과거분사'의 형태로 나타내며 계속, 완료, 경험, 결과의 네 가지의

쓰임이 있어요. 과거 문장은 과거의 사실만을 나타내지만, 현재완료 문장은 과거에서

현재까지 이어져 어떤 영향을 미치는지를 나타내요.

Unit 6

현재완료

1. 현재완료의 의미

과거에 일어난 일이 현재까지 영향을 미칠 때 현재완료 시제를 쓴다.

- 형태: have + 과거분사 (~한 적이 있다, ~해 왔다)

  He lived in the country. [과거] 그는 그 시골에 살았다.

  He lives in the city. [현재] 그는 그 도시에 산다.

  He has lived in Seoul since 2009. [현재완료] 그는 2009년 이후로 서울에 살고 있다.

2. 현재완료의 쓰임

현재완료는 계속, 완료, 결과, 경험의 4가지 의미를 나타낸다.

쓰임	의미 및 예문
〈계속〉 과거부터 현재까지 하고 있는 일	의미: (계속) ~해 왔다 ▶ How long ~?, for, since 등과 사용된다.
	I have been in Korea for two years. We have seen since 2007.
〈완료〉 과거부터 현재까지 해서 끝낸 일	의미: (벌써, 이미, 막) ~했다 ▶ just, already, yet 등과 사용된다.
	He has just finished his homework. They have not found the answer yet.

쓰임	의미 및 예문
〈경험〉 과거부터 현재까지 해 본 일	의미: ~한 적이 있다 ▶ before, once, ever, never 등과 사용된다.
	Have you ever been to Japan? I have eaten the food once.
〈결과〉 과거에 한 일의 결과가 현재에 남아 있는 일	의미: ~해 버렸다 (그래서 지금은 …다) ▶ lose, go, buy, come 등의 동사와 사용된다.
	He has gone to London. I have lost my watch.

have been to(~에 가 본 적이 있다)는 경험을, have gone to(~에 가 버렸다)는 결과를 나타낸다.

Pop Quiz Ⅰ. 다음 괄호 안에서 알맞은 것을 고르세요.
❶ I have (lost, lose) my watch. ❷ She has (went, gone) home.

3. 현재완료의 부정문과 의문문

(1) 현재완료의 부정문

형태: 주어＋have[has] not[never]＋과거분사

I haven't seen the movie yet. 나는 아직 그 영화를 못 봤다.

She has never been in America. 그녀는 미국에 가 본 적이 없다.

have not은 haven't로, has not은 hasn't로 줄여서 쓸 수 있다.

(2) 현재완료의 의문문

형태: (의문사)＋Have[Has]＋주어＋과거분사 ~?

Have you **ever** read **this book?** 이 책을 읽어 본 적이 있니?

Where has he **been?** 그는 어디에 있어왔니?

4. 현재완료와 과거시제

현재완료: 과거와 현재에 대한 정보를 동시에 나타낸다.

과거시제: 과거에 이미 끝난 일에 사용한다.(현재에 대해서는 알 수 없다.)

현재완료	과거
• 과거 일에 현재까지 영향을 미친 경우 (before, just와 함께 사용) I have finished the work. → 지금 막 끝냈음. He has played the violin for 2 years. → 과거에 시작해서 지금도 하고 있음. She has never played golf. → 과거부터 지금까지 경험을 나타냄. Ann has gone to New York. → 과거의 결과가 지금도 지속되어 있음.	• 과거에 일어난 일이 이미 끝난 경우 (ago, just now와 함께 사용) I finished the work. → 과거에 끝냈음. He played the violin 2 years ago. → 과거에는 했으나 지금은 알 수 없음. She didn't play golf yesterday. → 과거의 한 시점만을 나타냄. Ann went to New York. → 과거의 일을 나타내며 현재는 알 수 없음.

We visited Jeju Island last Summer. (○)

→ has visited (×)

yesterday, last night[week, month, year], ago, just now, when 명백한 과거를 나타내는 말들은 과거 시제에만 사용한다.

다음 빈칸에 주어진 동사의 과거분사 형태를 쓰세요.

1 cut _____

2 meet _____

3 win _____

4 get _____

5 send _____

6 take _____

7 bring _____

8 write _____

9 keep _____

10 tell _____

11 teach _____

12 sleep _____

13 quit _____

14 sit _____

15 build _____

16 know _____

17 make _____

18 become _____

19 lose _____

20 steal _____

21 see _____

22 are _____

23 go _____

24 stand _____

다음 주어진 동사의 과거형과 과거분사를 차례대로 쓰세요.

1 read – _____ – _____

2 sleep – _____ – _____

3 say – _____ – _____

4 sell – _____ – _____

5 put – _____ – _____

6 throw – _____ – _____

7 leave – _____ – _____

8 give – _____ – _____

9 rise – _____ – _____

10 drive – _____ – _____

11 catch – _____ – _____

12 fall – _____ – _____

13 swim – _____ – _____

14 run – _____ – _____

15 live – _____ – _____

16 find – _____ – _____

17 drink – _____ – _____

18 fight – _____ – _____

다음 주어진 동사를 이용하여 빈칸에 알맞은 동사의 형태를 쓰세요.

woods 숲

twice 두 번

complete 완성하다

1 I have _____ a snake in this woods. (see)

2 She has _____ her bag twice. (lose)

3 Kate has _____ to New York. (go)

4 How long have you _____ in Busan? (live)

5 Tom has _____ his homework. (finish)

6 We have already _____ our work. (complete)

7 Somebody has _____ my watch. (steal)

8 John has _____ his cell phone in the bus. (leave)

9 Amy hasn't _____ at the station yet. (arrive)

10 The kids have _____ the windows. (break)

11 Have you ever _____ before? (drive)

12 They have just _____ the wall. (paint)

13 We have _____ close friends since 2010. (be)

14 She has never _____ the museum. (visit)

15 He and his brother have _____ for ten hours. (sleep)

16 Dan has ever _____ a song on the stage. (sing)

다음 주어진 동사를 이용하여 현재완료 문장을 완성하세요.

diet 식이요법
falling 떨어지는
passport 여권
mailman 우체부

1 We _____ already _____ our lunch. (eat)

2 Jennifer _____ _____ on a diet since last week. (be)

3 The children _____ _____ a horse before. (ride)

4 He _____ not _____ the problem yet. (solve)

5 She _____ _____ for the bank for 20 years. (work)

6 I _____ _____ to China many times. (be)

7 Matt _____ _____ to his home country. (go)

8 _____ you ever _____ a falling star? (see)

9 He _____ already _____ the money. (spend)

10 _____ she _____ the artist before? (meet)

11 The old woman _____ _____ her passport. (lose)

12 We _____ just _____ at the building. (arrive)

13 The mailman _____ not _____ yet. (come)

14 It _____ _____ sunny since weekend. (be)

15 _____ you _____ a guitar lesson before? (take)

16 Mark and Bill _____ never _____ this town. (leave)

다음 문장을 축약형을 사용하여 부정문으로 바꾸어 다시 쓰세요.

tie 매다
textbook 교과서
ghost 유령

1 The girl has learned to tie the shoes.

   → _____

2 I have lost the textbook.

   → _____

3 Tom and Dan have seen a ghost.

   → _____

4 Sarah has finished her work.

   → _____

5 We have forgotten his name.

   → _____

6 They have cleaned the classroom.

   → _____

7 My parents have lived in New York.

   → _____

8 The boy has broken the window.

   → _____

9 I have worked at the museum.

   → _____

10 They have done the homework.

   → _____

다음 문장을 의문문으로 바꾸어 다시 쓰세요.

place 장소
project 계획, 설계
rainbow 무지개

I She has bought a new dress.

→ _____

2 Jonathan has gone to France.

→ _____

3 They have read the book before.

→ _____

4 Jenny has been in Japan for five years.

→ _____

5 You have lost my toy airplane.

→ _____

6 Amy has lived in many places.

→ _____

7 He has travel around the world.

→ _____

8 Jason has found his new job.

→ _____

9 They have already finished the project.

→ _____

10 You have seen a double rainbow before.

→ _____

다음 주어진 동사를 이용하여 빈칸에 현재완료나 과거시제로 쓰세요.

airport 공항
exhibition 전시회
wallet 지갑
flute 플루트

1 Jonathan _____ sick since last night. (be)

2 We _____ at the airport just now. (arrive)

3 He _____ me how to ride a bike yesterday. (teach)

4 They _____ the movie before. (see)

5 She _____ in this city for five years. (live)

6 We _____ each other since 2012. (know)

7 The man _____ an exhibition in 2008. (have)

8 When the phone _____, I slept on the bed. (ring)

9 He _____ to Canada twice. (be)

10 I _____ my wallet last month. (lose)

11 Tom _____ a robot for his son yesterday. (buy)

12 Julie _____ the flute for two years. (play)

13 When Judy _____ him, he was very busy. (visit)

14 My dad _____ soccer last Sunday. (play)

15 We _____ about you many times. (hear)

16 I _____ my computer last weekend. (sell)

다음 우리말과 같도록 빈칸에 알맞은 말을 넣어 문장을 완성하세요.

once 한 번

borrow 빌리다

1 그녀는 2008년 이후로 영어를 배우고 있다.

→ She _____ _____ English _____ 2008.

2 Harry는 막 그의 숙제를 끝마쳤다.

→ Harry _____ _____ _____ his homework.

3 너는 그 영화를 본 적이 있니?

→ _____ you _____ _____ the movie?

4 나는 전에 그 책을 읽은 적이 전혀 없다.

→ I _____ _____ _____ the book before.

5 우리는 오랫동안 서로를 알아 왔다.

→ We _____ _____ each other _____ a long time.

6 그들은 한 번 유럽에 가 본 적이 있다.

→ They _____ _____ to Europe _____.

7 너는 그녀를 얼마나 오래 만나 왔니?

→ How long _____ you _____ her?

8 그녀는 그 공원에서 그 사람을 보지 못했다.

→ She _____ _____ _____ the man in the park.

9 Tony가 벌써 나의 자전거를 빌려 갔다.

→ Tony _____ _____ _____ my bike.

10 나의 엄마는 5년 동안 수영을 해 오고 있다.

→ My mom _____ _____ _____ five years.

다음 우리말과 같도록 빈칸에 알맞은 말을 넣어 문장을 완성하세요.

drum 드럼
almost 거의
understand 이해하다

1 나는 드럼을 연주해 본 적이 있다.

→ I _____ _____ _____ the drum.

2 우리는 서울에서 5년 동안 살아왔다.

→ We _____ _____ in Seoul _____ five years.

3 우리 팀은 경기에서 이겨 본 적이 없다.

→ Our team _____ _____ _____ a game.

4 너는 전에 이 노래를 들어 본 적이 있니?

→ _____ you _____ this song _____?

5 그녀는 그녀의 나라로 떠나가 버렸다.

→ She _____ _____ _____ her country.

6 나는 거의 2년 동안 한국에 있었다.

→ I _____ _____ in Korea _____ almost two years.

7 Sally는 벌써 그녀의 방을 청소했다.

→ Sally _____ _____ _____ her room.

8 그는 일요일 이후로 계속 아팠다.

→ He _____ _____ sick _____ Sunday.

9 그는 그 문제를 아직 이해하지 못했다.

→ He _____ _____ _____ the question yet.

10 그녀는 8년 동안 과학을 가르쳐 왔다.

→ She _____ _____ science _____ eight years.

다음 빈칸에 알맞은 말을 쓰세요.

1 과거에 일어난 일이 현재까지 영향을 미칠 때 _____ 시제를 쓴다.

2 현재완료는 계속, 완료, 결과, 경험의 4가지 의미를 나타낸다.

쓰임	의미 및 예문
_____ 과거부터 현재까지 하고 있는 일	의미: (계속) ~해 왔다 ▶ How long ~?, for, since 등과 사용된다. I _____ _____ in Korea for two years. 나는 2년 동안 한국에 있어 왔다.
_____ 과거부터 현재까지 해서 끝낸 일	의미: (벌써, 이미, 막) ~했다 ▶ already, just, yet 등과 사용된다. He _____ _____ _____ his homework. 그는 그의 숙제를 막 끝냈다.
_____ 과거에 한 일의 결과가 현재에 남아있는 일	의미: ~해 버렸다 (그래서 지금은 …다) ▶ lose, buy, go, come 등의 동사와 사용된다. He _____ _____ to London. 그는 런던에 가버렸다.
_____ 과거부터 현재까지 해 본 일	의미: ~한 적이 있다 ▶ before, once, ever, never 등과 사용된다. _____ you _____ _____ to Japan? 너는 일본에 가 본 적이 있니?

3 과거와 현재에 대한 정보를 동시에 나타낼 때는 _____ 시제를 쓰며, 과거에 이미 끝난 일을 나타낼 때는 _____ 시제를 쓴다.

4 명백한 과거를 나타내는 말들은 _____ 시제에만 사용한다. → 과거를 나타내는 부사(구): _____ 어제, **last night** 지난밤, _____ 작년, _____ 지난, **just now** 방금, **when** 언제

다음 문장에서 밑줄 친 부분을 바르게 고쳐 쓰세요.

bill 계산서
dictionary 사전
backpack 배낭

1 We have <u>gone</u> to the zoo last week. → _____

2 She has <u>be</u> to Japan three times. → _____

3 They have already <u>pay</u> the bill. → _____

4 I <u>lost</u> my dictionary, so I don't have it. → _____

5 He have just <u>finish</u> writing the card. → _____

6 We <u>have moved</u> to this city ago. → _____

7 They have been married <u>since</u> ten years. → _____

8 Sally <u>has lost</u> her backpack yesterday. → _____

9 He has <u>saw</u> the pictures many times. → _____

10 It has rained <u>for</u> this morning. → _____

11 The boys <u>didn't have</u> had lunch yet. → _____

12 Have you ever <u>are</u> to New York? → _____

13 Matt <u>was</u> a teacher for fifteen years. → _____

14 My sister has <u>broke</u> my robot. → _____

15 Cathy has <u>climb</u> this mountain twice. → _____

16 I <u>have learned</u> how to swim last month. → _____

다음 〈보기〉와 같이 알맞게 배열하고 현재완료의 쓰임을 쓰세요.

golf 골프

〈보기〉
나는 그 뉴스를 들은 적이 없다.
(heard / I / the news / never / have)
→ I have never heard the news. (경험)

1 누군가 나의 자전거를 훔쳐갔다.
(my bike / stolen / somebody / has)
→ _____ (　　)

2 나는 1시간 동안 그녀를 기다리고 있다.
(her / one hour / I / waited for / for / have)
→ _____ (　　)

3 그들은 한 번 일본에 가 본 적이 있다.
(to Japan / they / been / have / once)
→ _____ (　　)

4 그는 막 그의 숙제를 끝냈다.
(has / his homework / he / just / finished)
→ _____ (　　)

5 너는 골프를 쳐 본 적이 있니?
(golf / ever / have / played / you)
→ _____ (　　)

6 우리는 아직 편지를 쓰지 않았다.
(yet / the letter / have / we / not / written)
→ _____ (　　)

다음 두 문장을 한 문장으로 바꿔 쓸 때 빈칸에 알맞은 말을 쓰세요.

subway 지하철
still 여전히
date 데이트를 하다

〈보기〉 He visited me last week. He is still staying with me.
→ He has stayed with me since last week.

I I lost my hat on the subway. I don't have my hat now.
→ _____ on the subway.

2 He lived in Seoul four years ago. He still lives there.
→ _____ four years.

3 Lucy went to New York. She isn't here now.
→ Lucy _____ .

4 Ann moved to Tokyo in 2011. She still lives in Tokyo.
→ Ann _____ .

5 The boy broke his leg. He is still hurt.
→ The boy _____ .

6 He left for China with his family. He isn't here now.
→ He _____ with his family.

7 Brian met Ashley last month. He still dated her.
→ Brian _____ last month.

8 Eric bought a new car in 2013. So he has it now.
→ Eric _____ 2013.

[1~3] 다음 중 빈칸에 알맞은 것을 고르세요.

1 My sister _____ to Canada, so she is not in Seoul.

① goes   ② is gone

③ have gone   ④ has gone

2 Nancy _____ finished her homework yet.

① doesn't   ② didn't have

③ has not   ④ have not to

3 They have met Jenny at the station _____.

① before   ② just now

③ yesterday   ④ last weekend

4 다음 대화의 괄호 안에 들어갈 말이 바르게 짝지어진 것을 고르세요.

> A: Have you (see) this movie?
> B: Yes, I (see) the movie two day ago.

① see – saw   ② seen – saw

③ seen – seen   ④ saw – seen

5 다음 빈칸에 공통으로 알맞은 것을 고르세요.

> · Peter _____ live in this town for ten years.
> · _____ Cathy already eaten lunch?

① have   ② has

③ did   ④ have not

6 다음 대화의 빈칸에 알맞지 <u>않은</u> 것을 고르세요.

> A: How long have you known Ann?
> B: _____

① Since 2005.

② For more than two years.

③ I have known her for six years.

④ It was three years ago.

7 다음 대화의 빈칸에 공통으로 들어갈 말을 쓰세요.

> A: Where have you _____?
> B: I have _____ in the park.

→ _____

8 다음 우리말과 같도록 빈칸에 알맞은 말을 쓰세요.

Tom은 5년 동안 뉴욕에 살고 있다.

= Tom _____ _____ in New York for five years.

9 다음 두 문장이 같은 뜻이 되도록 빈칸에 알맞은 말을 쓰세요.

Jane left for Japan, so she isn't here.

= Jane _____ _____ for Japan.

10 다음 밑줄 친 부분 중 어색한 것을 고르세요.

I ① <u>am lived</u> in Seoul ② <u>all my life</u>.

I ③ <u>have known good friends</u> ④ <u>for</u> a long time.

11 다음 〈보기〉의 밑줄 친 부분과 쓰임이 같은 것을 고르세요.

〈보기〉 She <u>has been</u> sick for a week.

① She <u>has seen</u> the movie once.
② I <u>have lost</u> my watch.
③ He <u>has</u> just <u>finished</u> his work.
④ We <u>have been</u> in London since last year.

12 다음 중 밑줄 친 부분의 쓰임이 다른 하나를 고르세요.

① He <u>has been</u> to China before.
② It <u>has rained</u> since last Sunday.
③ I <u>have seen</u> him many times.
④ He <u>has</u> never <u>visited</u> his uncle.

13 다음 괄호 안의 동사를 알맞은 형태로 바꾼 것을 고르세요.

The Korean War (break out) in 1950. I have heard of it since my childhood.

① break out   ② breaks out
③ broke out   ④ has broken out

14 다음 밑줄 친 부분 중 어색한 것을 고르세요.

① Kate <u>has stayed</u> there last month.
② He <u>has</u> already <u>washed</u> the car.
③ I <u>have painted</u> the pictures since 2012.
④ We <u>haven't been</u> late for school.

15 다음 밑줄 친 부분 중 올바른 것을 고르세요.

① He <u>have never seen</u> a snake before.
② I <u>have ever ate</u> spaghetti at the restaurant.
③ They <u>have worked</u> there last year.
④ They <u>have visited</u> the tower twice.

16 다음 밑줄 친 부분을 바르게 고친 것을 고르세요.

Susan <u>study</u> English since last year.

① studied   ② has studied
③ have studies   ④ 고칠 필요 없음.

[17~18] 다음 문장을 지시대로 바꾸어 쓰세요.

17 He has seen her since last Friday. (부정문)

→ _____

18 His brothers have bought him a present. (의문문)

→ _____

[19~20] 다음 두 문장을 한 문장으로 쓸 때 알맞은 말을 쓰세요.

19 I learned Chinese in 2012.
I still learn Chinese.

= I _____ Chinese since 2012.

20 She lost her bag last week.
She doesn't have it now.

= She _____ her bag since last week.

A 다음 그림을 보고, 현재완료와 just를 이용하여 문장을 완성하세요.

1 (eat)

2 (go)

3 (arrive)

1 They _____ _____ _____ the pizza.

2 All the students _____ _____ _____ home.

3 The woman _____ _____ _____ in Jeju Island.

B 다음은 Peter가 계획했던 일들입니다. 내용에 맞게 현재완료를 이용하여 문장을 완성하세요.

My Plan List		
things to do	**done**	**not done**
1. send an e-mail to Cathy	✓	
2. walk my dog		✓
3. clean my room with my brother	✓	
4. write a diary		✓

1 Peter _____ to Cathy.

2 Peter _____ dog.

3 Peter _____ .

4 Peter _____ .

Grammar Plus …?
시제

1. 현재시제

현재시제는 지금 벌어지고 있는 일을 말할 때 쓴다.

(1) 지속적인 현재 상태

   They live in Seoul now. 그들은 지금 서울에서 산다.

(2) 일상 생활에서 반복적인 일

   I get up early in the morning. 나는 아침에 일찍 일어난다.

(3) 불변의 진리, 사실

   Water freezes at 0℃. 물은 0℃에서 언다.

2. 과거시제

과거시제는 과거 이미 일어난 일을 말할 때 쓴다.

(1) 과거에 있었던 일이나 상태

   I was eleven years old last year. 나는 작년에 11살이었다.

(2) 역사적인 사실

   Edison invented the light bulb. Edison은 전구를 발명했다.

3. 미래시제

미래시제는 앞으로 하게 될 일이나 일어날 일을 말할 때 쓴다.

▶ 조동사 will이나 be going to를 사용해서 나타낸다.

He will visit you tomorrow. 그는 내일 너를 방문할 것이다.

= He is going to visit you tomorrow.

4. 진행시제

진행시제는 어떤 일이 일어나고 있는 중임을 나타내는 시제이다.

(1) 현재진행형: 지금 일어나고 있는 일

   I am reading a book at home. 나는 집에서 책을 읽고 있다.

(2) 과거진행형: 과거 한 시점에 일어나고 있던 일

   I was reading a book at home. 나는 집에서 책을 읽고 있었다.

(3) 미래진행형: 미래 한 시점에 일어나고 있을 일

   I will be reading a book at home. 나는 집에서 책을 읽고 있을 것이다.

현재완료 · **133**

■ A-B-C형 (원형, 과거형, 과거분사형이 각기 다른 형)

원형	과거형	과거분사
be (am, is)	was	been
be (are)	were	been
bear (낳다)	bore	born
begin (시작하다)	began	begun
bite (물다)	bit	bitten
blow (불다)	blew	blown
break (깨다)	broke	broken
choose (선택하다)	chose	chosen
do (하다)	did	done
draw (그리다)	drew	drawn
drink (마시다)	drank	drunk
drive (운전하다)	drove	driven
eat (먹다)	ate	eaten
fall (떨어지다)	fell	fallen
fly (날다)	flew	flown
forget (잊다)	forgot	forgotten
freeze (얼리다)	froze	frozen
give (주다)	gave	given
go (가다)	went	gone
grow (기르다, 자라다)	grew	grown
hide (숨다)	hid	hidden
know (알다)	knew	known
lie (눕다, 놓여 있다)	lay	lain
ride (타다)	rode	ridden
ring ((종을) 울리다)	rang	rung
rise (떠오르다)	rose	risen
see (보다)	saw	seen
shake (흔들다)	shook	shaken
show (보여주다)	showed	shown
sing (노래하다)	sang	sung
speak (말하다)	spoke	spoken
swim (수영하다)	swam	swum

take (얻다, 가지고 가다)	took	taken
tear (눈물 흘리다, 찢다)	tore	torn
throw (던지다)	threw	thrown
wear (입다)	wore	worn
write (쓰다)	wrote	written

■ A-B-B형 (과거형과 과거분사형이 같은 형)

원형	과거형	과거분사
bring (가져오다)	brought	brought
build (세우다)	built	built
buy (사다)	bought	bought
catch (잡다)	caught	caught
dig (파다)	dug	dug
feed (먹이를 주다)	fed	fed
feel (느끼다)	felt	felt
fight (싸우다)	fought	fought
find (찾다)	found	found
get (얻다)	got	got〔gotten〕
hang (매달다)	hung	hung
have (가지다)	had	had
hear (듣다)	heard	heard
hold (잡다)	held	held
keep (지키다, 유지하다)	kept	kept
lead (이끌다)	led	led
leave (떠나다)	left	left
lend (빌리다)	lent	lent
lose (잃다)	lost	lost
make (만들다)	made	made
mean (의미하다)	meant	meant
meet (만나다)	met	met
pay (지불하다)	paid	paid
say (말하다)	said	said
sell (팔다)	sold	sold

■ A-B-B형 (과거형과 과거분사형이 같은 형)

원형	과거형	과거분사
send (보내다)	sent	sent
sit (앉다)	sat	sat
sleep (자다)	slept	slept
spend (쓰다)	spent	spent
stand (서다)	stood	stood
strike (때리다)	struck	struck
teach (가르치다)	taught	taught
tell (말하다)	told	told
think (생각하다)	thought	thought
understand (이해하다)	understood	understood
win (이기다)	won	won
wind (감다)	wound	wound

■ A-B-A형 (원형과 과거분사형이 동일한 형)

원형	과거형	과거분사
become (~이 되다)	became	become
come (오다)	came	come
run (달리다)	ran	run

■ A-A-A형 (원형, 과거형, 과거분사형이 동일한 형)

원형	과거형	과거분사
cost ((돈이) 들다)	cost	cost
cut (자르다)	cut	cut
hit (치다)	hit	hit
hurt (다치다)	hurt	hurt
let (시키다)	let	let
put (놓다)	put	put
read[ri:d] (읽다)	read [red]	read [red]
set (설치하다)	set	set
shut (닫다)	shut	shut

수동태

수동태의 쓰임과 형태를 이해할 수 있다.

능동태 문장을 수동태 문장으로 만들 수 있다.

수동태에서 (by+행위자)를 생략하는 경우를 알 수 있다.

수동태 문장은 누가 무엇을 하는가가 아닌 어떤 일이 어떻게 일어나게 되었는지에 맞춰진

문장이에요. 그러므로 사물은 스스로 행동할 수 없기 때문에 사물이 주어인 경우에

수동태 문장을 사용할 때가 많은데, 수동태는 주어가 동사의 행위를 받는 대상일 때

사용해요.

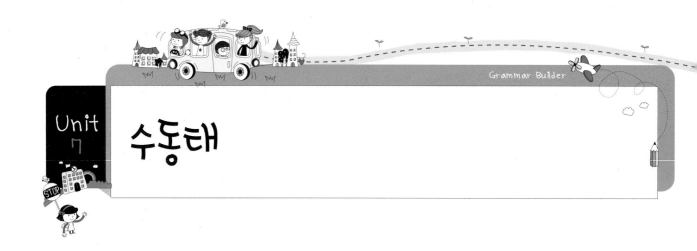

Unit 7

수동태

1. 능동태와 수동태

능동태는 동작을 하는 행위자에 중점을 둔 문장으로 행위자가 주어가 된다.

수동태는 무슨 일이 일어났는지에 중점을 둔 문장으로 대상이 주어가 된다.

> 능동태: ~가 …하다
> 수동태: ~가 …되다, 받다, 당하다
>   (be동사 + 과거분사 ~ by + 행위자)

Brian broke the window. [능동태] Brian이 창문을 깨뜨렸다.

행위자 → 누군가 행한 것에 중점

The window was broken by Brian. [수동태] 창문이 Brian에 의해 깨졌다.

일어난 일 → 행위자보다는 발생한 것에 중점

2. 수동태 만들기

I wrote the letter. 나는 그 편지를 썼다.

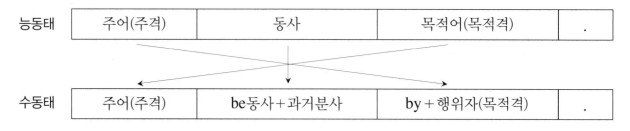

능동태	주어(주격)	동사	목적어(목적격)	.
수동태	주어(주격)	be동사 + 과거분사	by + 행위자(목적격)	.

The letter was written by me. 그 편지는 나에 의해 쓰여졌다.

수동태 만드는 법

1. 능동태의 목적어를 주어로 한다. (목적어 the letter가 주어가 된다.)

2. 동사를 'be동사+과거분사'의 형태로 고친다. 이때, 새로운 주어에 맞게 be동사를 사용한다. (wrote가 was written이 된다.)

3. 능동태의 주어를 'by+목적격'의 형태로 고친다.
   (주어 I가 by me가 된다.)

수동태로 바꿀 수 없는 경우
→ 동작의 대상이 되는 목적어가 수동태의 주어가 되므로 목적어가 없는 1, 2형식의 문장은 수동태로 만들 수 없다.

Pop Quiz   I. 다음 주어진 말을 알맞은 형태로 쓰세요.(현재시제)

❶ The bike _____ by him. (fix)

❷ This song _____ by them. (love)

3. 수동태의 시제

수동태의 현재와 과거시제는 be동사로 나타나고, 미래시제는 〈will+be+과거분사〉로 나타낸다.

The classroom is cleaned by students. [현재] 청소된다

Yesterday the room was cleaned by her. [과거] 청소되었다

The room will be cleaned by us tomorrow. [미래] 청소될 것이다

4. 조동사가 있는 수동태

조동사가 있는 수동태는 조동사 다음에 〈be+과거분사〉를 쓴다.

The problem can be solved by him. 해결될 수 있다

Animals should be protected by people. 보호되어져야 한다

5. 4형식 문장의 수동태

간접목적어와 직접목적어를 갖는 동사인 give, ask, tell, teach, show 등은 두 가지의 수동태를 만들 수 있다.

• 직접목적어를 주어로 하는 경우, 간접목적어 앞에 전치사(to, for, of)를 써 준다.

My father gave me some apples.

→ I was given some apples by my father. [간접목적어 주어]

→ Some apples were given to me by my father. [직접목적어 주어]

My father bought me a bike.

→ A bike was bought for me by my father.

make, buy, get 등의
동사는 직접목적어를
주어로 하는
수동태만 만든다.

6. by+행위자를 생략하는 경우

수동태 문장에서 〈by+행위자〉를 생략할 수가 있는데 by them, by us, by people 등은 거의 생략하는 경우가 많다.

❶ 행위자가 일반적인 사람일 때

Stars are seen at night (by people). 별들은 밤에 보인다.

English is spoken in America (by Americans). 영어는 미국에서 사용된다.

❷ 행위자를 모르거나 중요하지 않을 때

The window was broken (by someone). 그 창문이 깨졌다.

Pop Quiz　　2. 다음 주어진 말을 알맞은 형태로 쓰세요.

❶ The poem _____ by her yesterday. (write)

❷ This park will _____ by us tomorrow. (visit)

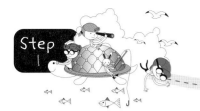

다음 주어진 동사의 과거분사를 쓰세요.

1 make _____

2 hurt _____

3 build _____

4 read _____

5 invent _____

6 say _____

7 teach _____

8 see _____

9 cut _____

10 take _____

11 send _____

12 steal _____

13 know _____

14 eat _____

15 write _____

16 paint _____

17 buy _____

18 give _____

19 keep _____

20 break _____

21 speak _____

22 show _____

23 ride _____

24 throw _____

다음 괄호 안에서 알맞은 것을 골라 동그라미 하세요.

1 This play (was written, wrote) by Shakespeare.

2 He (built, was built) the building two years ago.

3 The boxes (is carried, are carried) by him.

4 The letter will (be, was) sent by the woman.

5 Stars (see, are seen) at night by us.

6 You can (finish, be finish) the work.

7 I (was bought, bought) the computer yesterday.

8 The window (broke, was broken) by someone.

9 The test will be (gave, given) tomorrow.

10 The telephone (invented, was invented) by Bell.

11 They (read, were read) the books then.

12 The Wright brothers (made, were made) an airplane.

13 The classroom (clean, is cleaned) by the students.

14 Many fish (are eaten, ate) by two cats.

15 We (ordered, were ordered) the food.

16 A mouse (killed, was killed) by the snake.

play 연극

order 주문하다

다음 괄호 안의 동사를 이용하여 문장을 완성하세요.

architect 건축가
discover 발견하다
missing 실종된

1 The church _____ by the architect ago. (build)

2 Anne Frank _____ the diary then. (write)

3 America _____ by Columbus. (discover)

4 I _____ in Seoul in 2003. (bear)

5 The blue jeans _____ by German. (make)

6 Sunglasses _____ by many people now. (wear)

7 Pablo Picasso _____ the pictures. (paint)

8 The boys _____ by Mr. Smith last year. (teach)

9 The star will _____ again. (see)

10 The vase _____ by the kid yesterday. (break)

11 The man will _____ the letter soon. (deliver)

12 Hemingway _____ *The Old Man and Sea*. (write)

13 The pictures _____ by my brother last week. (take)

14 English _____ in the US. (speak)

15 This park _____ by us yesterday. (visit)

16 The police _____ the missing child last night. (find)

다음 우리말과 같도록 주어진 단어를 이용하여 문장을 완성하세요.

perfume 향수
destroy 파괴하다
fee 요금
post 게시하다

1 그 자전거는 Peter에 의해 수리될 것이다. (repair)

→ The bike _____ _____ _____ _____ Peter.

2 이 헬멧들은 그 사람들에 의해 사용되었다. (use)

→ This helmets _____ _____ _____ the people.

3 저 향수는 젊은 여자들에 의해 사랑받는다. (love)

→ That perfume _____ _____ _____ young women.

4 많은 집들은 그 허리케인에 의해 파괴되었다. (destroy)

→ Many houses _____ _____ _____ the hurricane.

5 그 차들은 사람들에 의해 운전될 것이다. (drive)

→ The cars _____ _____ _____ _____ people.

6 그 요금은 카드로 지불될 수 있다. (pay)

→ The fee _____ _____ _____ _____ credit card.

7 그 음악은 그 유명한 밴드에 의해 연주되었다. (play)

→ The music _____ _____ _____ the famous band.

8 그 비싼 신발은 Jennifer에 의해 만들어졌다. (make)

→ The expensive shoes _____ _____ _____ Jennifer.

9 그 공은 Max에 의해 바구니에 던져졌다. (throw)

→ The ball _____ _____ into the basket _____ Max.

10 그 사진은 Sally에 의해 어제 게시되었다. (post)

→ The photo _____ _____ _____ Sally yesterday.

다음 문장을 주어진 말로 시작하여 수동태로 바꿔 다시 쓰세요.

professor 교수
park 주차하다

I Everyone loved Mary and Amy.

→ Mary and Amy _____.

2 Jill cleans these rooms every day.

→ These rooms _____.

3 The students respected the professor.

→ The professor _____.

4 She made her sons some cookies.

→ Some cookies _____.

5 John parked the car in the street.

→ The car _____.

6 Many people read this novel each year.

→ This novel _____.

7 People learn English all over the world.

→ English _____.

8 She gave us some apple juice.

→ We _____.

9 My father bought me a new bike.

→ A new bike _____.

10 Many people use the subway every day.

→ The subway _____.

다음 문장을 주어진 말로 시작하여 수동태로 바꾸어 쓰세요.

message 메시지
checklist 점검표

1 Brian told them a funny story.
→ They _____ .
→ A funny story _____ .

2 Susan sent Mark a long message.
→ Mark _____ .
→ A long message _____ .

3 The students ask him a question.
→ He _____ .
→ A question _____ .

4 Thomas gave her a diamond ring.
→ She _____ .
→ A diamond ring _____ .

5 Mr. Brown teaches them science.
→ They _____ .
→ Science _____ .

6 The doctor sent her a health checklist.
→ She _____ .
→ A health checklist _____ .

7 My brother made me spaghetti.
→ Spaghetti _____ .

8 Billy bought her a concert ticket.
→ A concert ticket _____ .

다음 문장을 수동태 문장으로 바꾸어 다시 쓰세요.

fence 울타리, 담
thick 두꺼운
ladder 사다리
play 연극

1 Amy sent the postcard last Monday.

→ _____

2 Cathy loves the red roses.

→ _____

3 They invited the children.

→ _____

4 My mom cleaned the bathroom.

→ _____

5 She drew the picture yesterday.

→ _____

6 Jonathan will paint the fence.

→ _____

7 Shakespeare wrote the play.

→ _____

8 The little boy can read the thick book.

→ _____

9 Dan and Tom carried the ladder.

→ _____

10 A Frenchman made the Statue of Liberty.

→ _____

다음 문장을 수동태 문장으로 바꾸어 다시 쓰세요.

scary 무서운
secretary 비서
brick 벽돌
wild 야생의

1 The director made this scary movie.

→ _____

2 The kids ate some cookies and candies.

→ _____

3 Your father will help your sister.

→ _____

4 People see the moon at night.

→ _____

5 The secretary can copy the book.

→ _____

6 The farmer built the brick house.

→ _____

7 They protected the wild animals.

→ _____

8 The children broke the windows.

→ _____

9 Thomas Edison invented the light bulb.

→ _____

10 Everyone loves Alice and Lucy.

→ _____

다음 문장을 능동태 문장으로 바꾸어 다시 쓰세요.

mayor 시장

match 경기

cancel 취소하다

1 The bears are caught by the hunters.

→ _____

2 The cars were washed by the man.

→ _____

3 Credit cards are used by many people.

→ _____

4 Ashley's purse was stolen by a thief.

→ _____

5 The park was visited by the mayor.

→ _____

6 Some sandwiches were made for us by dad.

→ _____

7 These bags were made by Ann and Joe.

→ _____

8 Soccer matches are loved by them.

→ _____

9 A CD player was bought for me by her.

→ _____

10 The meeting was canceled by us.

→ _____

다음 빈칸에 알맞은 말을 쓰세요.

1 _____는 동작을 하는 행위자에 중점을 둔 문장으로 행위자가 주어가 된다. 반면, _____는 무슨 일이 일어났는지에 중점을 둔 문장으로 대상이 주어가 된다.

2 **수동태 만드는 법**

(1) 능동태의 _____를 주어로 한다.

(2) 동사를 'be동사+_____'의 형태로 고친다. 이때, 새로운 주어에 맞게 be동사를 사용한다.

(3) 능동태의 주어를 'by+_____'의 형태로 고친다.

I wrote the letter. → (수동태) _____

3 동작의 대상이 되는 목적어가 수동태의 주어가 되므로 목적어가 없는 _____, _____형식의 문장은 수동태로 만들 수 없다.

4 수동태의 현재와 과거시제는 _____동사로 나타나고, 미래시제는 _____+_____+과거분사로 나타낸다.

5 조동사가 있는 수동태는 조동사 다음에 _____+_____를 쓴다.

6 간접목적어와 _____를 갖는 4형식 문장은 두 가지의 수동태를 만들 수 있다. 단, make, buy, get 등의 동사는 _____를 주어로 하는 수동태만 만든다.

7 수동태 문장에서 1. 행위자가 일반적인 사람일 때, 2. 행위자를 모르거나 중요하지 않을 때 _____ +_____를 생략할 수 있다.

다음 문장에서 밑줄 친 부분을 바르게 고쳐 다시 쓰세요.

reveal 드러나다
puzzle 퍼즐
robber 강도

1 The story *Snow White* is <u>loving</u> by kids. → _____

2 The room will <u>is</u> cleaned by Amy. → _____

3 Shakespeare <u>was written</u> *Hamlet*. → _____

4 The wall was painted <u>with</u> the men. → _____

5 The silver ring was found by <u>she</u>. → _____

6 A thief <u>was stolen</u> my new bike. → _____

7 The telephone was <u>invent</u> by Bell. → _____

8 The cars <u>was</u> stopped by the people. → _____

9 The secret will be <u>reveal</u> by him. → _____

10 The pink dress was given <u>Jane</u> by me. → _____

11 The puzzle can <u>solve</u> by you. → _____

12 The dog was <u>saving</u> by the brave man. → _____

13 Her songs <u>was</u> loved by everyone. → _____

14 My grandfather is <u>grown</u> apple trees. → _____

15 The robber was <u>catch</u> by the police. → _____

16 Mickey Mouse was <u>creating</u> by Walt Disney.

→ _____

Jump Up 3

다음 문장에서 틀린 부분을 찾아 바르게 고쳐 문장을 다시 쓰세요.

elect 선출하다
prize 상
compose 작곡하다
wrong 잘못된

1 Spanish is spoke in Mexico by people.

→ _____

2 David was electing our class leader.

→ _____

3 He will is given a special prize by us.

→ _____

4 A computer were bought to me by my mother.

→ _____

5 My brother was found the key on the bed.

→ _____

6 The music is composed last month with her.

→ _____

7 The camera was given for him by us.

→ _____

8 Coffee is growing in hot countries by people.

→ _____

9 She was sent the letter to the wrong address.

→ _____

10 Korean food will is ordering by them.

→ _____

다음 우리말과 같도록 주어진 단어를 이용하여 영어로 쓰세요.

package 소포
arrest 체포하다
connect 연결하다
chase 쫓다

1 초콜릿은 그 어린이들에 의해 사랑받는다. (love, chocolate)

→ _____

2 그 엘리베이터는 그에 의해 수리될 것이다. (elevator, repair)

→ _____

3 그 소포는 그 우편배달부에 의해 배달되었다. (package, deliver)

→ _____

4 신선한 야채들이 그들에 의해 제공되었다. (fresh, serve)

→ _____

5 그 야생 동물들은 그 사냥꾼에 의해 잡혔다. (wild, catch)

→ _____

6 우리는 Ann에 의해 파티에 초대받았다. (invite, party)

→ _____

7 미국은 Columbus에 의해 발견되었다. (America, discover)

→ _____

8 한 도둑은 그 여자에 의해 어제 체포되었다. (thief, arrest)

→ _____

9 그 도시들은 그 열차에 의해 연결될 것이다. (connect, will)

→ _____

10 그 강도는 그 젊은 남자들에 의해 쫓긴다. (robber, chase)

→ _____

[1~2] 다음 중 문장의 빈칸에 알맞은 것을 고르세요.

1 The pants _____ by my mother.
① washed
② was washed
③ were washed
④ to be washed

2 Sally's birthday party _____ next Friday.
① is held
② was held
③ will hold
④ will be held

[3~4] 다음 우리말과 같도록 괄호 안의 동사를 이용하여 완성하세요.

3
> 그 편지는 Peter에 의해 쓰여졌다.
> → The letter _____ by Peter. (write)

→ _____

4
> 그 창문이 Tom에 의해 깨졌다.
> → The window _____ by Tom. (break)

→ _____

5 다음 두 문장의 의미가 같도록 빈칸에 알맞은 것을 고르세요.

> The man gave me red roses.
> = Red roses _____ me by the man.

① are given at
② were given to
③ are given to
④ were given for

6 다음 대화의 밑줄 친 부분의 알맞은 형태를 고르세요.

> A: Who painted the *Mona Lisa*?
> B: It painted by Leonardo da Vinci.

① was painted
② to paint
③ was painting
④ is painted

7 다음 밑줄 친 부분 중 생략할 수 있는 것을 고르세요.
① Your ball was found by her.
② It is made in Korea by them.
③ The bus was driven by Brian.
④ The actor is loved by kids.

8 다음 문장을 수동태로 바르게 바꾼 것을 고르세요.

> My father bought me a bike.

① I was bought a bike by my father.
② A bike was bought to me by my father.
③ A bike was bought for me by my father.
④ I was bought a bike for me by my father.

9 다음 중 어법상 어색한 것을 고르세요.
① The work will be done tomorrow.
② I was born in Canada.
③ Spanish is spoken in Spain.
④ We are teaching math by him.

10 다음 중 의미가 나머지와 다른 하나를 고르세요.
① Julia gave me a pretty doll.
② I gave Julia a pretty doll.
③ I gave a pretty doll to Julia.
④ Julia was given a pretty doll by me.

[11~12] 다음 괄호 안에서 알맞은 단어를 고르세요.

11 The book (reads / is read) by people.

12 They (helped / are helped) by the student.

[13~14] 다음 주어진 단어를 활용하여 능동태, 수동태 문장을 완성하세요.

13 Thomas Edison / invent / the light bulb
→ The light bulb _____
_____.

→ Thomas Edison _____
_____.

14 Leo Tolstoy / the book *War and Peace* / write
→ The book *War and Peace* _____
_____.

→ Leo Tolstoy _____
_____.

A 다음 그림을 보고, 수동태 표현을 이용하여 문장을 완성하세요.

1 The kangaroo wears boxing gloves.

→ Boxing gloves _____ .

2 Some boys saw the scary movie.

→ The scary movie _____ .

B 다음 표를 보고, 〈보기〉와 같이 완전한 문장으로 쓰세요.

인물	한 일
Leonardo da *Vinci*	painted the *Mona Lisa*
the Wright Brothers	invented airplanes
O. Henry	wrote *The Last Leaf*

〈보기〉　The *Mona Lisa* was painted by Leonardo da *Vinci*.

1 Airplanes _____ .

2 *The Last Leaf* _____ .

Unit 8

관계대명사

관계대명사의 의미와 쓰임을 이해할 수 있다.

관계대명사의 종류와 역할을 알고 활용할 수 있다.

문장에서 관계대명사가 생략 가능한 경우를 알 수 있다.

관계대명사는 두 문장을 하나로 연결하는 접속사이면서도 앞에 나온 명사를 대신하는 대명사의 역할을 해요. 관계대명사가 이끄는 문장이 설명해 주는 대상, 즉 선행사에 따라 관계대명사가 달라져요. 선행사가 사람일 때는 관계대명사 who가, 동물이나 사물일 때에는 which가 와요.

Unit 8 관계대명사

1. 관계대명사의 의미

관계대명사는 두 문장을 하나로 이어주는 접속사 역할과 명사를 대신하는 대명사의 역할을 동시에 한다.

I know a woman.	+	She plays the piano well.
나는 한 여자를 안다.		그녀는 피아노를 잘 친다.

→ I know a woman, <u>and she</u> plays the piano well. [접속사+대명사]

→ I know <u>a woman</u> <u>who</u> plays the piano well. 나는 피아노를 잘 치는 한 여자를 안다.
　　　　　선행사　관계대명사

> 관계대명사 바로 앞에 있는 명사나 대명사를 선행사라고 하며 관계대명사는 이 선행사를 가리키는 말이다.

2. 관계대명사의 쓰임

관계대명사는 대명사처럼 주격, 소유격, 목적격이 있다. 선행사가 사람일 때는 관계대명사 who가, 동물이나 사물일 때는 which가, 사람이나 동물, 사물일 때는 that이 온다.

선행사/격	주격	소유격	목적격
사람	who	whose	whom(who)
사물, 동물	which	of which, whose	which
사람, 사물, 동물	that	–	that

(1) 주격 관계대명사

· 관계대명사가 이끄는 절에서 관계대명사가 주어를 대신하는 경우에 쓴다.

I like the man. + He is a good actor.

→ I like the man <u>who</u> is a good actor. [주격]
　　　선행사(사람) (= the man) 나는 훌륭한 배우인 그 남자를 좋아한다.

The book is fun. + It was about cooking.

→ The book <u>which</u> was about cooking is fun. [주격]
　　　선행사(사물) (= the book) 요리에 관한 그 책은 재미가 있다.

Pop Quiz

I. 다음 who와 which 중 알맞은 것을 쓰세요.

❶ He is the man _____ helped me then.

❷ This is the hat _____ she bought.

(2) 소유격 관계대명사

· 관계대명사가 이끄는 절에서 관계대명사가 소유의 의미인 경우에 쓴다.

I know a man. + His name is Jack.

→ I know a man <u>whose</u> name is Jack. [소유격]
　　　선행사(사람) (= his) 나는 이름이 Jack인 한 남자를 안다.

Look at the lion. + Its color is white.

→ Look at the lion <u>whose</u> color is white. [소유격]
　　　선행사(동물) (= its)

> 선행사가
> 사물 또는 동물이 때,
> 〈whose+명사〉 또는
> 〈of which+명사〉 둘 다
> 쓸 수 있지만 of which는
> 거의 쓰지 않는다.

(3) 목적격 관계대명사

· 관계대명사가 목적어를 대신하는 경우에 쓴다.

This is the girl. + I like her.

→ This is the girl <u>whom[who]</u> I like. [목적격]
　　　선행사(사람)　(= her) 이 사람은 내가 좋아하는 소녀이다.

I have the letter. + You sent it last week.

→ I have the letter <u>which</u> you sent last week. [목적격]
　　　선행사(사물)　(= it) 나는 네가 지난주에 보낸 그 편지를 가지고 있다.

주격 관계대명사 뒤에는
동사가 오고,
목적격 관계대명사 뒤는
주어가 온다.

3. 관계대명사 that

관계대명사 that은 who(m)나 which 대신에 쓰인다. 단, 선행사가 최상급, 서수, -thing, -body 또는 '사람＋동물'일 때는 that만 쓴다.

Look at the boy and his dog. + They are running.

Look at <u>the boy and his dog</u> <u>that</u> are running.
　　　　선행사(사람＋동물)　　　달리고 있는 그 소년과 그의 개를 봐라.

4. 관계대명사의 생략

〈주격 관계대명사＋be동사〉와 〈목적격 관계대명사〉는 생략이 가능하다.

The boy (who is) crying is my brother. 울고 있는 그 소년은 내 동생이다.

This is the girl (whom) I met yesterday. 이 소녀는 내가 어제 만난 소녀이다.

Pop Quiz　**2.** 다음 괄호 안에서 알맞은 것을 고르세요.

❶ I have a book (that / whose) cover is blue.

❷ There is something (which / that) I need to tell you.

다음 문장에서 선행사에 ○를, 관계대명사에 △를 하세요.

roof 지붕

necklace 목걸이

deep 깊은

1 I love that girl who is reading on the sofa.

2 I have a friend whose father is a scientist.

3 This is the boy who I introduced to you before.

4 He is the only foreigner that I know.

5 He gave me the pen which he bought yesterday.

6 The park which is near his house is wonderful.

7 She lives in a big house whose roof is green.

8 This is the girl whom I saw in the park.

9 Look at the girl and her dog that are walking there.

10 The woman who is in the kitchen is my mom.

11 The necklace which she is wearing is expensive.

12 This is all the money that I have.

13 That is the bike that my father bought me.

14 There is a child whose name is Jack.

15 The lake which is in this town is very deep.

16 They have a car whose color is blue.

다음 괄호 안에서 알맞은 것을 골라 동그라미 하세요.

1 The girl (who, which) is in the hall is my sister.

2 They check everything (that, who) they need.

3 We saw a man and his parrot (who, that) are talking.

4 I still have the watch (which, who) he gave me.

5 She wore the dress (who, which) he bought her.

6 We ate the food (who, which) Sally cooked.

7 This is all the pencils (who, that) I have.

8 There is a woman (who, whose) name is Cathy.

9 This is the boy (whom, who) came from China.

10 The jacket (which, whose) she is wearing is new.

11 It is a game (who, that) is popular in Korea.

12 He liked the movie (which, whom) he saw twice.

13 There is a man (whose, who) is a good swimmer.

14 I know the girl (whose, whom) dog was missing.

15 I like the books (which, whom) have good pictures.

16 This is Jason (whose, whom) I met in the park.

hall 강당

parrot 앵무새

popular 인기있는

swimmer
수영하는 사람

다음 문장의 주어에는 ○표를, 동사에는 △표를 하세요.

language 언어
famous 유명한

1 The man likes Sarah who he met at the party.

2 The actor whom I wanted to see was at the cafe.

3 We met the woman whose brother knew us.

4 They saw the people whose car broke down.

5 We know a girl who can speak four languages.

6 They have a house whose roof is yellow.

7 Julia wore a hat that was too big for her.

8 The man who is in the hall is my uncle.

9 The bag which I carried was very heavy.

10 They were the men who invented an airplane first.

11 John lost the pen that she gave him.

12 I like the sweater which my friend is wearing.

13 The man who lives next door is a teacher.

14 Do you have the money that she gave you?

15 The people who we met last Sunday were kind.

16 I know the woman whose sister is a famous singer.

다음 문장에서 생략할 수 있는 부분에 밑줄을 그으세요.

thank 감사하다
person 사람
eagle 독수리

1 The books which are on the desk are mine.

2 This is the bag which my mother bought me.

3 I still have the ring which you gave me.

4 The boy who is on the playground is my brother.

5 He lived in a house which is painted green.

6 The man who is driving the truck is Kevin.

7 The player thanked them who were cheering for him.

8 He is the person whom I called yesterday.

9 Eat the food which was cooked by Cathy.

10 I found the restaurant which you look for.

11 The people who I work with are very nice.

12 Do you know the student who Ann is talking to?

13 The movie which they watched was very funny.

14 There are eagles which are flying in the sky.

15 Have you found the purse which you lost?

16 Look at the lion which is running after the deer.

다음 괄호 안에서 알맞은 동사의 형태를 골라 문장을 완성하세요.

zebra 얼룩말
fridge 냉장고
healthy 건강한

1 There is a zebra which (is, are) running there.

2 The letters which (is, are) on the table is hers.

3 I like Sue and Lucy who (are, be) kind.

4 The person who (live, lives) next door is a pilot.

5 There is a boy who (is, are) good at swimming.

6 Where is the cake that (was, were) in the fridge?

7 I know the men who (help, helps) other people.

8 People who exercise every day (is, are) healthy.

9 Those pencils which (is, are) in the room are his.

10 He likes the book which (have, has) many photos.

11 Look at the boy and the dog that (is, are) running.

12 She has a car whose color (is, are) yellow.

13 The park which is near my house (is, are) clean.

14 We know a man who (play, plays) soccer well.

15 The bike that I bought yesterday (are, is) stolen.

16 The people who (work, works) here are very nice.

Step I

Check Up 6

다음 빈칸에 알맞은 관계대명사를 쓰세요. (who의 목적격은 whom 으로 쓰고, that은 that을 써야 하는 경우에만 쓰세요.)

1 He liked her _____ he met at the party.

2 We packed the things _____ we needed for a trip.

3 Bell was the man _____ invented the telephone.

4 I saw a boy and a dog _____ were running there.

5 The scientist _____ I like most is Albert Einstein.

6 I saw a pretty girl _____ has long hair.

7 We met a friend _____ father is a cook.

8 Is this the book _____ Brian read last week?

9 You are the only one _____ trust me.

10 She is the girl _____ helped the child yesterday.

11 I know the boy _____ dog was missing.

12 They bought everything _____ they needed.

13 The radio _____ he gave me was very nice.

14 We know the girl _____ mother is a lawyer.

15 This is all the money _____ I have in my pocket.

16 I saw a cat _____ tail was very short.

pack 꾸리다
cook 요리사
trust 믿다
everything 모든 것
lawyer 변호사

다음 두 문장을 관계대명사를 이용해 한 문장으로 만드세요.

theater 극장
scarf 스카프

1   They ate the food. It was cooked by her.

→ _____

2   The man is Billy. We saw him in the theater.

→ _____

3   I still have the teddy bear. You gave me it.

→ _____

4   There is a boy. His name is Peter.

→ _____

5   Tom is wearing blue jeans. They are new.

→ _____

6   Do you know the girl? Tom is walking with her.

→ _____

7   The scarf is very expensive. Lisa is wearing it.

→ _____

8   She is a teacher. I met her yesterday.

→ _____

9   Look at the girl and her dog. They are running.

→ _____

10 I like the computer. Brian is using it now.

→ _____

Step 2 — Build Up 2

다음 두 문장을 관계대명사를 이용해 한 문장으로 만드세요.

1 I live in a new house. Its roof is brown.

→ _____

2 I know the children. Their father is a police officer.

→ _____

3 The people are very kind. She met them last night.

→ _____

4 I like Picasso. His paintings are unique.

→ _____

5 We packed the things. We needed them for camping.

→ _____

6 I know the girl. She can speak three languages.

→ _____

7 This is a woman. She came from Canada.

→ _____

8 Ann was carrying a bag. It was very light.

→ _____

9 I see a little boy. He is riding a donkey.

→ _____

10 Look at the lion. It is running after the deer.

→ _____

police officer
경찰관

unique 독특한

camping 캠핑

light 가벼운

donkey 당나귀

Build Up 3

다음 두 문장을 관계대명사를 이용해 한 문장으로 다시 만드세요.

frog 개구리
pianist 피아니스트
orchard 과수원

1 The house was built in 2000. It is in the picture.

→ _____

2 The frog is his. It jumps two meters high.

→ _____

3 He married a woman. She was from French.

→ _____

4 This is a storybook. It is good for children.

→ _____

5 I met a girl. Her mother is a famous pianist.

→ _____

6 This is the mountain. I took nice pictures there.

→ _____

7 This is the best book. I have ever read it.

→ _____

8 The watch made in the US. I bought it.

→ _____

9 The apples are sweet. They grow in my orchard.

→ _____

10 I gave her all the money. I have the money.

→ _____

다음 빈칸에 알맞은 말을 쓰세요.

1 관계대명사는 두 문장을 하나로 이어주는 _____ 역할과 명사를 대신하는 _____의 역할을 동시에 한다.

2 관계대명사 바로 앞에 있는 _____나 대명사를 _____라고 한다.

3 관계대명사는 대명사처럼 주격, 소유격, _____이 있다. 선행사가 사람일 때는 관계대명사 _____가, 동물이나 사물일 때는 _____가, 사람이나 동물, 사물일 때는 _____이 온다.

선행사 / 격	주격	소유격	목적격
사람	_____	_____	whom(who)
사물, 동물	_____	whose, of which	_____
사람, 사물, 동물	_____	–	_____

4 소유격 관계대명사의 경우, 선행사가 사물 또는 동물일 때, _____+명사 또는 of which+명사 둘 다 쓸 수 있지만 of which는 거의 쓰지 않는다.

5 주격 관계대명사 who와 목적격 관계대명사 who를 구별하는 방법은 주격 관계대명사 뒤에는 _____가 오고, 목적격 관계대명사 뒤는 _____가 온다.

6 관계대명사 _____은 who(m)나 which 대신 쓰인다. 단, 선행사가 최상급, 서수, -thing, -body 또는 '_____+동물'일 때는 _____만 쓴다.

7 〈주격 관계대명사+_____〉와 〈_____ 관계대명사〉는 생략 가능하다.

다음 문장에서 밑줄 친 부분을 바르게 고쳐 쓰세요.

eyesight 시력
bite 물다
professor 교수

1　There is a child <u>who</u> eyesight is good.　→ _____

2　I have a dog <u>whose</u> doesn't bite people.　→ _____

3　He is a man <u>which</u> came from Italy.　→ _____

4　I will visit Amy that <u>live</u> in New York.　→ _____

5　There is something <u>which</u> I forgot.　→ _____

6　Judy is wearing a coat <u>who</u> I like.　→ _____

7　People who exercise regularly <u>is</u> healthy.　→ _____

8　There was a girl <u>that</u> name was Cinderella. → _____

9　I love the painter <u>whose</u> painted that.　→ _____

10　He is the only man <u>who</u> solved it.　→ _____

11　This is the dog <u>who</u> helped the man.　→ _____

12　It is the biggest car <u>which</u> I have ever seen. → _____

13　I saw a rabbit <u>which</u> ears was very big.　→ _____

14　We have a friend <u>who</u> mom is a professor.　→ _____

15　Do you know the man <u>whose</u> Ann likes?　→ _____

16　I told him something <u>which</u> surprised him. → _____

다음 두 문장을 관계대명사가 있는 문장과 생략한 문장으로 각각 쓰세요.

stage 무대
borrow 빌리다

1 Look at the boys. They are singing on the stage.

→ _____

→ _____

2 The toys are made in Japan. They are in the box.

→ _____

→ _____

3 He is the kind man. She gave him the key.

→ _____

→ _____

4 This is the picture. It was painted by my sister.

→ _____

→ _____

5 The coffee smells good. I bought it from London.

→ _____

→ _____

6 He can borrow the books. They are in my room.

→ _____

→ _____

7 He is my son. He is talking with them.

→ _____

→ _____

다음 우리말과 같도록 괄호 안에 주어진 단어를 알맞게 배열하세요.

subject 과목

sharp 날카로운

1 영어는 내가 가장 좋아하는 과목이다.

(like, that, the subject, is, I, most)

→ English _____.

2 나는 뛰어가는 그 소년과 그의 개를 안다.

(and, that, are, the boy, running, his dog)

→ I know _____.

3 그녀는 날카로운 이빨을 가진 고양이를 가지고 있다.

(sharp, that, a cat, has, teeth)

→ She has _____.

4 그는 그 문제에 답할 수 있는 학생이다.

(the question, can, a student, answer, who)

→ He is _____.

5 나는 그의 이름이 Peter라는 한 소년을 찾고 있다.

(a boy, is, looking for, whose, name, Peter)

→ I am _____.

6 이것은 내가 어제 잃어버린 가방과 똑같다.

(yesterday, I, the same, lost, bag)

→ This is _____.

7 나는 지붕에 작은 창문들이 있는 집에 산다.

(small, roof, house, windows, has, whose)

→ I live in the _____.

8 우리가 샀던 집은 언덕 위에 있다.

(is, which, we, on, bought, the hill)

→ The house _____.

[1~2] 다음 중 문장의 빈칸에 알맞은 것을 고르세요.

1 This is the table _____ I made two days ago.
① who   ② whose
③ whom   ④ which

2 We met an old man _____ hair was gray.
① who   ② whose
③ whom   ④ which

[3~4] 다음 문장에서 어색한 부분을 찾아 바르게 고쳐 쓰세요.

3

> The people who work in the office looks happy.

_____ → _____

4

> These are the books whose I borrowed from the library.

_____ → _____

5 다음 빈칸에 공통으로 알맞은 것을 고르세요.

> · He is the boy _____ stole your wallet.
> · He likes stories _____ have happy endings.

① who   ② which
③ that   ④ whose

6 다음 두 문장을 한 문장으로 바꿀 때 빈칸에 알맞은 말을 쓰세요.

> The meal was very good.
> We cooked it.
> → The meal _____ _____ _____ was very good.

→ _____

7 다음 밑줄 친 부분의 쓰임이 〈보기〉와 같은 것을 고르세요.

> 〈보기〉 The dress that she is wearing is beautiful.

① The man that I saw was tall.
② That boy is my brother.
③ I think that you are honest.
④ This is shorter than that.

8 다음 밑줄 친 부분과 바꾸어 쓸 수 있는 것을 고르세요.

> I'm looking for the pen <u>which</u> my dad bought for me.

① who   ② where
③ whom   ④ that

9 다음 중 밑줄 친 부분의 쓰임이 나머지와 다른 것을 고르세요.

① <u>Who</u> do you meet there?
② I like Judy <u>who</u> helps me.
③ He is the boy <u>who</u> is kind.
④ We met the woman <u>who</u> came from the US.

10 다음 빈칸에 that이 들어갈 수 <u>없는</u> 것을 고르세요.

① This is the best book _____ I have ever read.
② A girl and a cat _____ are playing together are there.
③ The necklace _____ he bought made in Japan.
④ I met a girl _____ father was a pilot.

[11~12] 괄호 안에서 알맞은 관계대명사를 고르세요.

11 The man (which / who) lives next door is a dancer.

12 The park (who / which) is near my home is good.

[13~14] 다음 주어진 문장을 관계대명사 who 나 which를 이용하여 한 문장으로 만드세요.

13 Do you know the woman? + She took care of animals.

→ _____

_____

14 He is an actor. The actor stars in a lot of movies.

→ _____

_____

A 다음 그림을 보고, 첫 번째 빈칸에는 그림의 번호를 쓰고, 두 번째 빈칸에는 관계대명사를 쓰세요.

① pilot

② peach

③ vet

1 A _____ is someone _____ treats sick animals.

2 A _____ is a fruit _____ has white or yellow flesh with a hard seed at the center.

3 A _____ is someone _____ flies an airplane.

B 다음 한 문장을 두 문장으로 바꾸어 쓰세요.

1 The boy is my friend who can speak Chinese.

→ _____

2 An elephant is an animal which has a very long nose.

→ _____

[1~4] 다음 중 빈칸에 알맞은 동사의 형태를 고르세요.

1 I have something _____ you.
① give   ② gives
③ to give   ④ giving

2 I like _____ a piano lesson.
① take   ② took
③ to taking   ④ taking

3 Thank you for _____ me at the party.
① inviting   ② to invite
③ to inviting   ④ invite

4 Mark decided _____ a car.
① buy   ② to buy
③ bought   ④ buying

5 다음 문장에서 to부정사가 명사적 쓰임으로 사용된 것을 고르세요.
① They have many things to do.
② Peter studied hard to pass the test.
③ My hobby is to collect stamps.
④ He was so surprised to see her.

6 다음 〈보기〉와 to부정사의 쓰임과 같은 것을 고르세요.

〈보기〉 I want some water to drink.

① I'm happy to meet you.
② It's time to say goodbye.
③ We decided where to go.
④ She wants to work more.

7 다음 주어진 동사와 동사의 현재분사의 짝이 바르지 않은 것을 고르세요.
① smile – smiling
② walk – walking
③ stop – stopping
④ dance – danceing

8 다음 우리말을 영어로 바르게 옮긴 것을 고르세요.

> 나는 그 문을 열었던 것을 기억한다.

① I remember opening the door.
② I remember to open the door.
③ I regret opening the door.
④ I regret to open the door.

9 다음 〈보기〉와 동명사의 쓰임이 같은 것을 고르세요.

> My job is selling books.

① Playing soccer is very fun.
② My favorite activity is fishing.
③ I can't stop laughing.
④ James gave up taking the test.

10 다음 중 빈칸에 들어갈 말이 다른 것을 고르세요.

① She teaches science _____ us.
② I sent an e-mail _____ Brian.
③ Ann bought a watch _____ him.
④ He gave a ring _____ Lisa.

11 다음 문장의 빈칸에 들어갈 알맞은 말을 고르세요.

> The old man _____ of me.

① ask some questions
② made spaghetti
③ bought new toys
④ often told funny stories

12 다음 중 밑줄 친 부분이 잘못된 것을 고르세요.

① The lemons tastes sour.
② The roses smell greatly.
③ The voice sounds good.
④ Cathy looks beautiful today.

13 다음 문장의 빈칸에 공통으로 알맞은 것을 고르세요.

> She cooked a cake _____ them.
> John made a big kite _____ me.

① of   ② to
③ with   ④ for

[14~15] 다음 문장의 빈칸에 알맞은 것을 고르세요.

14 He has _____ finished the work.

① already   ② yet

③ before   ④ since

15 We have lived _____ ten years.

① since   ② yet

③ during   ④ for

16 다음 현재완료의 쓰임이 〈보기〉와 같은 것을 고르세요.

> 〈보기〉   Somebody has stolen my bike.

① Have you ever been to China?

② The childs has seen the tiger before.

③ He has gone to his house.

④ Tom and his friends have swum for many years.

17 우리말과 같도록 빈칸에 알맞은 말을 쓰세요.

> I have _____ left this town.
> 나는 이 마을을 떠나 본 적이 없다.

→ _____

18 다음 문장이 수동태 문장이 되도록 빈칸에 알맞은 것을 고르세요.

> Hangeul _____ by King Sejong.

① invents

② invented

③ was invented

④ had invented

19 다음 문장을 수동태 문장으로 바꿔 쓸 때, 빈칸에 알맞은 말을 쓰세요.

The students respect the professor.

→ The professor _____

_____.

20 다음 두 문장을 한 문장으로 바꿔 쓸 때, 빈칸에 알맞은 말을 쓰세요.

I know the man. + He is an actor.

→ _____

_____.

Final Test 2

[1~3] 다음 문장의 빈칸에 들어갈 수 <u>없는</u> 것을 고르세요.

1 I _____ to go to see a movie.

① enjoyed   ② hoped

③ decided   ④ liked

2 We didn't know _____.

① where to go

② when to go

③ to go

④ what to do

3 Jane _____ doing her work.

① finished   ② wanted

③ postponed   ④ gave up

4 다음 우리말과 같도록 빈칸에 알맞은 말을 쓰세요.

> 저 소파는 편안해 보인다.
> = That sofa _____ comfortable.

→ _____

5 다음 중 to부정사의 형용사적 쓰임으로 쓰인 것을 고르세요.

① He came <u>to help</u> us.

② I like <u>to go</u> to church.

③ I don't know how <u>to go</u> there.

④ We have a lot of food <u>to eat</u>.

6 다음 중 to부정사의 부사적 쓰임으로 쓰인 것을 고르세요.

① My dream is <u>to be</u> a singer.

② He has something <u>to hide</u>.

③ There is no water <u>to drink</u>.

④ She was glad <u>to get</u> a house.

7 다음 중 밑줄 친 부분의 쓰임과 같은 것을 고르세요.

> <u>Making</u> a cake is very fun.

① The <u>smiling</u> baby is cute.

② He admitted <u>breaking</u> a vase.

③ My brother is <u>singing</u> a song.

④ They are <u>watching</u> TV now.

8 John sent a letter _____ her.
① to   ② of
③ for   ④ with

9 He asked her address _____ us.
① to   ② of
③ for   ④ with

10 She made a cake _____ me.
① to   ② of
③ for   ④ with

11 다음 두 문장이 같도록 빈칸에 알맞은 것을 고르세요.

To keep a diary is very hard.
= _____ is very hard to keep a diary.

① This   ② That
③ It   ④ Who

12 다음 중 to부정사의 쓰임이 다른 하나를 고르세요.
① I hate to sleep in the dark.
② They liked to drink soda.
③ They want to go to the zoo.
④ I am sorry to hear the news.

13 다음 중 밑줄 친 부분의 쓰임이 나머지와 다른 것을 고르세요.
① My hobby is playing soccer.
② She was playing the piano.
③ The barking dog is mine.
④ There are many shining stars.

14 다음 중 동사와 과거분사의 짝이 올바르지 않은 것을 고르세요.
① be – been
② break – broken
③ know – known
④ sleep – sleep

15 다음 현재완료 문장이 되도록 빈칸에 알맞은 말을 고르세요.

> Have you ever _____ before?

① swim   ② swam

③ swum   ④ swimming

[16~17] 다음 현재완료의 쓰임이 나머지와 다른 것을 고르세요.

16 ① I have been sick since Sunday.

② Ann has played tennis for two years.

③ How long have you known him?

④ I have already cleaned my room.

17 ① I have eaten the food once.

② She has never been to the US.

③ The men haven't arrived yet.

④ Have you ever traveled by airplane?

18 다음 우리말과 같도록 빈칸에 알맞은 것을 고르세요.

> 두 도시는 그 기차들에 의해 연결되었다.
> = Two cities _____ by the trains.

① were connected

② were connecting

③ was to connect

④ have connected

19 다음 문장을 수동태 문장으로 바꿔 쓰세요.

The hunters catch the bears.

→ _____

20 다음 두 문장을 연결할 때 빈칸에 알맞은 것을 고르세요.

> The story is interesting.
> You wrote the story yesterday.
> → The story _____ you wrote yesterday is interesting

① who   ② whose

③ which   ④ what

중등 영어 문법 실력 쌓기!

Grammar Builder

5

Answer Key

Answer Key

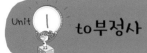

Unit 1 to부정사

Pop Quiz

1. ❶ to play ❷ To sing
2. ❶ to lend ❷ to buy

■ Step 1 | Check Up 1   p. 17

1. to eat 2. to do 3. to make 4. to buy
5. to pass 6. to see 7. to borrow 8. to meet
9. to protect 10. to go 11. to drink 12. to read
13. to be 14. to do 15. to learn 6. To exercise

■ Step 1 | Check Up 2   p. 18

1. houses 2. a computer 3. many books
4. water 5. a new piano 6. a lot of food
7. nothing 8. some cookies 9. a big room
10. something 11. time 12. any plan
13. some paper 14. many things 15. the way
16. many places

■ Step 1 | Check Up 3   p. 19

1. to hear 2. to buy 3. to be 4. to see
5. to study 6. to leave 7. to get 8. to take
9. to meet 10. to help 11. to do 12. To read
13. to be 14. to go 15. to solve 16. to use

■ Step 1 | Check Up 4   p. 20

1. to snow 2. to meet 3. to do 4. to play

5. to buy 6. to use 7. to see 8. to get
9. to exercise 10. to make

■ Step 1 | Check Up 5   p. 21

1. to collect 2. to buy 3. to give 4. to like
5. to eat 6. to hear 7. to travel 8. to go
9. to finish 10. to live

■ Step 1 | Check Up 6   p. 22

1. to live 2. to get 3. to sleep 4. how to use
5. to study 6. to be 7. where to go
8. to have[eat] 9. what to do 10. To love

■ Step 2 | Build Up 1   p. 23

1. He was very pleased to see her.
2. There was no water to drink.
3. They found a place to hide.
4. We wanted to see a movie tonight.
5. We promised not to be late.
6. He didn't know where to put the box.
7. It is hard to pass the exam.
8. I need onions to make this dish.

■ Step 2 | Build Up 2   p. 24

1. Please tell me how to use the machine.
2. I have something to give you.
3. My dream is to be a vet.
4. Jack went to a store to buy sneakers.
5. It is boring to talk about the same things.
6. I have some money to buy the car.
7. It is necessary to take a music lesson.

8. Dan asked me what to cook.

■ Step 2 l Build Up 3   p. 25

1. It, to swim 2. It, to remember 3. It, to ask
4. It, to understand 5. It, to break 6. where to put
7. when to open 8. how to use 9. what to cook
10. how to get 11. what to do 12. where to go

■ Step 3 l Jump 1   p. 26

1. 동사원형, 형용사, 동사 2. 주어, 목적어, 보어
3. 단수, 주어, it 4. not, not 5. 명사, 형용사
6. 부사, 목적, 원인
7. 의문사, 명사, what, where, when, how

■ Step 3 l Jump 2   p. 27

1. to bake 2. to see 3. not to 4. clean 5. be
6. is 7. to do 8. to save 9. to meet 10. to be
11. to swim 12. to hear 13. to travel 14. drive
15. take 16. It

■ Step 3 l Jump 3   p. 28

1. is to climb 2. want to go 3. how to use
4. money to buy 5. surprised to see
6. is to become 7. when to move
8. radio to listen 9. difficult to cut
10. friends to play

■ Step 3 l Jump 4   p. 29

1. hear the news.
2. He must be a fool to believe the rumor.
3. He went to the store to buy a bike.
4. Lisa went to Canada to learn English.
5. Cathy bought a magazine to read.
6. Tom drove to my school to pick me up.
7. They were glad to receive a letter from him.
8. I need a new shirt to put on.

9. To eat late at night is bad for your health.
10. Bill has many books to read this week.

■ Step 4 l 실전 평가   p. 30

1. ④ 2. ① 3. ③ 4. ④ 5. ② 6. ③ 7. ② 8. ③
9. ② 10. to buy some fruit
11. surprised to see someone in the dark 12. ③
13. ① 14. ② 15. ① 16. ④ 17. ② 18. ①
19. to play with 20. ④

1. 의문사와 to부정사가 결합하여 문장에서 명사처럼 사용
   되며 '~해야 할지'라는 뜻으로 how to는 '~하는 방법
   을'로 해석한다.
2. '~에 살 집이 없다'라는 뜻으로 전치사 in이 필요하다.
3. to부정사가 주어일 경우, 주어가 길어지는 것을 피하기
   위해 it을 주어로 삼고 to부정사를 문장 뒤로 보낼 수
   있다.
4. '나에게 질문할 문제들'이라는 뜻으로 to ask로 사용해
   야 한다.
5. ②번은 to부정사가 명사 뒤에 와서 형용사 역할을 하며
   명사를 수식하는 형용사적 쓰임이고 나머지는 부사적
   쓰임이다.
6. ③번을 제외한 나머지는 to부정사가 문장에서 명사 역
   인 주어, 목적어, 보어로 쓰여 명사적 쓰임이다. ③번은
   부사적 쓰임으로 목적을 나타낸다.
7. to부정사의 부정은 to부정사 앞에 not을 붙인다.
9. '달에서 걸은 첫 번째 사람'이라는 뜻으로 to부정사가
   와야 한다.
13. '저것을 들어서 슬프다'는 뜻으로 to부정사가 부사 역
    할을 하며 동사나 형용사를 수식하고 있다.
14. ②번은 날씨에 주어로 사용된 비인칭 주어 it이고 나
    머지는 to부정사가 주어가 길어서 뒤로 빼고 앞에 사
    용된 가주어 it이다.
15. ①번은 to 부정사가 뒤에서 명사를 수식하는 형용사적
    쓰임으로 to show가 되어야 한다.
16. 파이 만드는 방법은 how to make a pie로 나타낸
    다.

17. '경기에 이겨서 기뻤다'라는 뜻으로 to부정사의 부사적 쓰임(to win the race)으로 나타내야 한다.

18. ②번은 To play가 되어야 한다. 또한 to부정사 뒤에는 항상 동사원형이 온다. ③번은 to buy가 되어야 한다.

20. '보는 것이 믿는 것'이라는 뜻으로 to부정사인 to believe가 명사 역할을 하고 있어 명사적 역할을 하고 있는 것을 찾으면 된다. ④번은 '나의 꿈은 무대에서 노래를 부르는 것'이라고 명사 역할을 하고 있다.

■ Step 5 | 서술형 평가   p. 32

A **1.** angry to find a bug in the soup.
   2. sad to say goodbye to them.
   3. glad to receive many flowers.
B **1.** hope to get better grades
   2. wish to become healthier
   3. want to make new friends

Unit 2 동명사

Pop Quiz
Ⅰ. ❶ Playing ❷ helping
2. ❶ to dance ❷ doing

■ Step 1 | Check Up 1   p. 37

1. Sending **2.** collecting **3.** talking **4.** doing

5. inviting **6.** Playing **7.** taking **8.** Learning
9. watching **10.** snowing **11.** Driving **12.** flying
13. opening **14.** drinking **15.** cooking
16. speaking

■ Step 1 | Check Up 2   p. 38

1. surfing **2.** to read **3.** calling **4.** taking
5. selling **6.** jogging **7.** to watch **8.** to meet
9. Keeping **10.** riding **11.** to help **12.** taking
13. meeting **14.** seeing **15.** to swim **16.** being

■ Step 1 | Check Up 3   p. 39

1. making **2.** to go **3.** answering **4.** to be
5. to eat **6.** having **7.** living **8.** doing
9. traveling **10.** to help **11.** Standing **12.** taking
13. cleaning **14.** to go **15.** to pass **16.** to go

■ Step 1 | Check Up 4   p. 40

1. to buy **2.** stealing **3.** skiing **4.** reading
5. getting **6.** painting **7.** to use **8.** to send
9. being **10.** to swim **11.** to go **12.** to find
13. locking **14.** riding **15.** watching **16.** meeting

■ Step 1 | Check Up 5   p. 41

1. studying **2.** to wash **3.** playing **4.** to fly[flying]
5. raining **6.** answering **7.** to come **8.** smoking
9. to leave **10.** breaking **11.** waiting **12.** inviting
13. to look **14.** preparing **15.** opening
16. to make[making]

■ Step 1 | Check Up 6   p. 42

1. swimming **2.** traveling **3.** asking **4.** to buy
5. moving **6.** to play **7.** answering **8.** hiding
9. to be **10.** to stand **11.** coughing **12.** to visit
13. going **14.** being **15.** to wait
16. to read[reading]

1. avoided answering   2. started raining[to rain]
3. happy to meet   4. is getting[to get]
5. like to do   6. continued working[to work]
7. shop to buy   8. is playing[to play]
9. hospital to see   10. decided to keep
11. considered moving

1. kept looking for   2. began crying[to cry]
3. admitted breaking   4. enjoy driving
5. wants to be   6. hate studying[to study]
7. gave up making   8. decided to bake
9. stopped dancing   10. hope to climb
11. loves writing[to write]

1. cooking   2. to close   3. Saving[To save]
4. to plant   5. inviting   6. playing   7. to meet
8. to go   9. Riding[To ride]   10. Learning[To learn]
11. breaking   12. reading[to read]   13. talking
14. losing

1. 동명사, ing   2. 명사, 목적어   3. 하는 것은, 단수, it
4. 동명사   5. 동명사   6. to부정사   7. 동명사, to부정사
8. ~했던 것을 기억하다

1. Keeping[To keep]   2. moving   3. coming
4. to meet   5. talk   6. taking   7. to be   8. packing
9. swimming   10. bite   11. visiting   12. making
13. to lose   14. to fight   15. wear   16. working

1. Learning a computer is not diffcult.

2. She didn't give up making cookies.
3. Recycling bottles is very important.
4. Thomas decided to leave the town.
5. Swimming in the deep water is dangerous.
6. Watching too much TV is not good.
7. Making a speech in English is easy.
8. The children hope to go to the gallery.

1. to be   2. give up   3. to move   4. to break
5. is playing   6. to use   7. to go   8. doing
9. finding   10. to help   11. Swimming is

1. ③   2. ②   3. ④   4. ①   5. ④   6. breaking   7. ②
8. ①   9. ③   10. ②   11. ③   12. ①   13. ④   14. ②, ③
15. ①   16. ③   17. ④   18. skate → skating

1. 동사이면서 명사의 역할을 한다고 해서 동명사라고 하며, 형태는 동사 뒤에 -ing를 붙이며 문장에서 주어, 목적어, 보어로 쓰인다.
2. 동사의 종류에 따라 동명사를 목적어로 쓰거나, to부정사를 목적어로 쓰는데 consider는 동명사를 목적어로 쓴다.
3. 전치사 뒤에는 명사가 오는데, 동사가 올 경우에는 동명사의 형태로 쓴다.
4. 목적어에 to부정사가 있는 것으로 보아, 동명사를 목적어로 쓰는 avoid는 올 수 없다.
5. 목적어에 동명사가 있는 것으로 보아, to부정사를 목적어로 쓰는 wish는 올 수 없다.
6. enjoy, finish, give up, stop, postpone, admit, avoid, imagine, consider, keep은 목적어로 동명사를 쓰는 동사이다.
7. want, plan, hope, decide, offer, promise, agree, learn, forget, fail은 목적어로 to부정사를 쓰는 동사이다.
8. '~을 잘한다'라는 뜻은 be good at을 사용하여 나타

낸다. 또한 전치사 at 뒤에는 동명사가 와야 한다.

9. promise는 목적어로 to부정사를 쓰는 동사이다.

12. want는 to부정사를 목적어로 쓰는 동사로 to play가 들어간다.

13. continue는 동명사나 to부정사를 모두 목적어로 취하는 동사이다. 그러므로 practicing 또는 to practice 가 되어야 한다.

14. love는 목적어로 동명사와 to부정사를 모두 취할 수 있는 동사로 빈칸에는 cooking과 to cook이 들어갈 수 있다.

15. like, love, hate, begin, start, continue, bother는 목적어로 동명사나 to부정사를 모두 목적어로 취하는 동사이다.

16. finish, imagine, avoid 다음에는 목적어로 동명사가 온다.

17. plan, hope 다음에는 목적어로 to부정사가 온다.

■Step 5 | 서술형 평가   p. 52

A **1.** We finished doing our homework yesterday.

 2. She hopes to find a four-leaf clover in the garden.

 3. Sally gave up trying to go on a diet during the vacation.

B **1.** listening[to listen] to music, reading[to read] books

 2. making model cars

 3. playing with my dog, getting[to get] up early

Unit 3 **현재분사와 과거분사**

Pop Quiz

1. ❶② ❷②
2. ❶ boring ❷ excited

■Step 1 | Check Up 1   p. 59

1. walking, walked **2.** hitting, hit
3. smiling, smiled **4.** stopping, stopped
5. bringing, brought **6.** having, had
7. reading, read **8.** playing, played
9. going, gone **10.** dancing, danced
11. planning, planned **12.** thinking, thought
13. giving, given **14.** opening, opened
15. buying, bought **16.** eating, eaten

■Step 1 | Check Up 2   p. 60

1. studied **2.** slept **3.** let **4.** understood
5. stayed **6.** thrown **7.** washed **8.** put
9. bit **10.** forgotten **11.** made **12.** visited
13. meant **14.** spoken **15.** listened **16.** said
17. paid **18.** stood **19.** planned **20.** stolen
21. stopped **22.** had **23.** read **24.** taken
25. cut **26.** covered **27.** cried **28.** danced
29. risen **30.** told **31.** run **32.** thought

■Step 1 | Check Up 3   p. 61

1. been **2.** felt **3.** smiled **4.** forgiven **5.** cost
6. shut **7.** worried **8.** flown **9.** lost **10.** sat
11. broken **12.** loved **13.** passed **14.** begun
15. built **16.** gotten **17.** come **18.** pushed **19.** fed
20. known **21.** quit **22.** swum **23.** looked
24. hung **25.** rode **26.** taught **27.** done **28.** heard
29. drawn **30.** hidden **31.** drunk **32.** hit

1. lent 2. set 3. been 4. fought 5. become
6. carried 7. written 8. sung 9. fallen 10. kept
11. played 12. found 13. brought 14. frozen
15. met 16. spent 17. bought 18. given
19. walked 20. gone 21. chosen 22. grown
23. caught 24. tried 25. sent 26. baked
27. rung 28. won 29. finished 30. worn
31. seen 32. left

Step 1 । Check Up 5   p. 63

1. looking 2. talking 3. called 4. waiting 5. tired
6. interesting 7. crossing 8. closed 9. sitting
10. lost 11. walking 12. written 13. standing
14. covered 15. playing 16. planted

Step 1 । Check Up 6   p. 64

1. 현재분사 2. 동명사 3. 현재분사 4. 동명사
5. 동명사 6. 현재분사 7. 현재분사 8. 동명사
9. 현재분사 10. 현재분사 11. 동명사 12. 동명사
13. 현재분사 14. 동명사 15. 동명사 16. 현재분사

Step 2 । Build Up 1   p. 65

1. given 2. running 3. drawing 4. broken
5. holding 6. sleeping 7. riding 8. fallen
9. baked 10. staying 11. invited 12. burning
13. borrowed 14. spent 15. born 16. walking

Step 2 । Build Up 2   p. 66

1. flying 2. broken 3. standing 4. written
5. interesting 6. traveling 7. cooked 8. swimming
9. shining 10. called 11. washing 12. closed
13. smiling 14. worried 15. sleeping 16. hidden

Step 2 । Build Up 3   p. 67

1. surprised 2. disappointing 3. shocked

4. boring 5. interested 6. exciting 7. surprising
8. tiring 9. satisfied 10. bored 11. disappointed
12. depressed 13. satisfying 14. confused
15. shocking 16. excited

Step 3 । Jump 1   p. 68

1. ing, 진행 2. (1) 진행형 (2) 명사 (3) 보어
3. ed, 불규칙, 수동 4. (1) 명사 (2) 보어
5. 형용사, 현재, 과거 6. ing, 형용사, 명사

Step 3 । Jump 2   p. 69

1. covered 2. interested 3. swimming 4. rising
5. sleeping 6. broken 7. running 8. living
9. exciting 10. written 11. stolen 12. surprised
13. floating 14. moving 15. talking 16. made

Step 3 । Jump 3   p. 70

1. interesting, interested 2. exciting, excited
3. satisfied, satisfying 4. surprising, surprised
5. tired, tiring 6. disappointing, disappointed
7. confused, confusing 8. shocking, shocked

Step 3 । Jump 4   p. 71

1. man playing the piano
2. is a used computer
3. likes baked onions
4. those barking dogs
5. an amazing story it is
6. bike parked by the door
7. the burning building
8. satisfied with her grade
9. picture hung on the wall
10. of the sleeping baby

Step 4 । 실전 평가   p. 72

1. ② 2. ③ 3. stood → standing

4. throwing → thrown **5.** ④ **6.** ① **7.** ① **8.** ③

9. ② **10.** ④ **11.** working **12.** injured **13.** taking

14. lost **15.** ④ **16.** frightening, frightened

1. 현재분사는 〈동사원형+-ing〉의 형태로, '~하는, ~하고 있는'의 뜻으로 명사 앞이나 뒤에서 형용사처럼 명사를 수식한다. '빨간 모자를 쓴 그 소녀'라는 뜻으로 뒤에서 명사를 수식하고 있다.

2. 과거분사는 〈동사원형+-ed〉 또는 〈불규칙 변화〉 형태로, '~된, ~받는'의 뜻으로 수동과 완료를 나타내며, 여기서는 '훔친 자전거'라는 뜻이다.

3. '큰 나무 앞에 서 있는 소년을 좋아한다'라는 뜻으로 과거분사가 아닌 현재분사가 와야 한다.

4. 숲으로 던져진 완료 상태를 나타내므로 과거분사가 와야 한다.

5. 분사는 명사 앞에서 수식하지만, 수식어구와 함께 쓰이면 명사 뒤에서 수식한다. 여기서는 말하고 있는 상태를 나타내므로 현재분사가 와야 한다.

6. 누군가에 의해 쓰인 책이므로 과거분사인 written이 와야 한다.

7. surprise, interest, excite 등 사람의 감정을 나타낸 동사가 현재분사나 과거분사로 쓰여 문장에서 형용사 역할을 하는데, 주로 현재분사는 사물이 주어이거나 사물을 수식할 때, 과거분사는 사람이 주어이거나 사람을 수식할 때 쓰인다.

8. 〈보기〉의 문장은 형용사 역할로 명사를 꾸며주는 현재분사이다. ③번을 제외한 나머지는 명사 역할로 쓰인 동명사이다.

9. '덮여져 있는 산'이라는 뜻으로 과거분사인 covered가 와야 한다.

11. 현재분사는 '~하고 있는, ~하는'의 능동과 진행을 나타낸다.

12. 과거분사는 '~하된, ~받는'의 수동과 완료를 나타낸다.

13. 현재분사는 be동사와 함께 진행형을 만든다.

15. 셔츠는 스스로 행동을 하는 주인이 될 수 없다. 그러므로 과거분사 형태가 들어간다.

16. 감정을 주는 주체는 -ing를 쓰고, 감정을 받는 대상은 -ed를 쓴다.

■ **Step 5 ǀ 서술형 평가**　　　　　　　　　　p.74

A **1.** like baked corns **2.** running on the bus

　3. The man lying under the tree

B confused, worrying, surprising, surprised, boring, bored, exciting, excited, shocking, shocked, interesting, interested

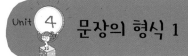

Unit **4**　문장의 형식 1

Pop Quiz

1. ❶S-The frog, V-jumps ❷S-My father, V-is

2. ❶3 ❷5

■ **Step 1 ǀ Check Up 1**　　　　　　　　　　p.79

1. S-We, V-met **2.** S-The sun, V-rises

3. S-Jack and you, V-are **4.** S-My friend, V-sent

5. S-His behavior, V-made

6. S-He and she, V-are **7.** S-They, V-are

8. S-The leaves, V-become **9.** S-John, V-played

10. S-My teacher, V-asked

11. S-The greedy man, V-smiles

12. S-The soldiers, V-dig

13. S-The young woman, V-gave

14. S-A big bird, V-flew

■ Step 1 ı Check Up 2 p. 80

1. C-the leader 2. C-good men

3. O-the vegetables 4. C-white and big

5. O-TV 6. O-books 7. C-good

8. O-the pictures 9. C-sleepy 10. C-sick

11. O-Brian 12. O-the window 13. C-sour

14. O-a nice dress

■ Step 1 ı Check Up 3 p. 81

1. V-made, C-a movie star 2. V-painted, C-green

3. V-thinks, C-smart 4. V-makes, C-comfortable

5. V-called, C-Pluto 6. V-make, C-dirty

7. V-found, C-difficult 8. V-made, C-wet

9. V-think, C-touching 10. V-made, C-beautiful

11. V-call, C-a walking dictionary

12. V-found, C-interesting

13. V-named, C-Tony

14. V-advised, C-to exercise

■ Step 1 ı Check Up 4 p. 82

1. My brother made me angry.

2. The teacher asked us a question.

3. They give me useful information.

4. Judy and Kate found the box empty.

5. The man bought her the flowers.

6. Sally wrote her parents a letter.

7. English people call elevators lifts.

8. The prince gave them the treasure.

9. We should keep the earth clean.

10. Brian sent me a lot of e-mails.

■ Step 2 ı Build Up 1 p. 83

1. 목적어 2. 간접목적어 3. 동사 4. (목적격) 보어

5. 보어 6. 목적어 7. 동사 8. 주어 9. 직접목적어

10. 간접목적어 11. 보어 12. 간접목적어 13. 동사

14. 주어 15. 보어 16. 목적어

■ Step 2 ı Build Up 2 p. 84

1. 1 2. 5 3. 2 4. 3 5. 5 6. 4 7. 3 8. 1 9. 5

10. 3 11. 2 12. 1 13. 4 14. 2 15. 3 16. 5

■ Step 2 ı Build Up 3 p. 85

1. 3 2. 1 3. 5 4. 4 5. 1 6. 5 7. 2 8. 4 9. 1

10. 2 11. 3 12. 4 13. 2 14. 1 15. 5 16. 1

■ Step 3 ı Jump 1 p. 86

1. 주어, 동사, 목적어, 보어, 수식어 2. 주어, 동사

3. 주어, 동사, 보어, 형용사, 형용사

4. 주어, 동사, 목적어, 명사

5. 간접목적어, 직접목적어, 사람, 사물, 수여

6. 목적어, 목적격 보어, 형용사, to부정사

■ Step 3 ı Jump 2 p. 87

1. S-The bear, V-sleeps, 1

2. S-His mother, V-made, O-him, C-a doctor, 5

3. S-Kevin, V-wrote, O-a letter, 3

4. S-His story, V-sounds, C-strange, 2

5. S-The children, V-play, 1

6. S-Peter, V-bought, O-his son, O-a toy, 4

7. S-Everyone, V-thinks, O-Linda, C-smart, 5

8. S-This iced coffee, V-tastes, C-good, 2

9. S-I, V-gave, O-my girlfriend, O-a gift, 4

10. S-We, V-think, O-him, C-a police officer, 5

11. S-My mother, V-baked, O-some cookies, 3

12. S-They, V-went, 1

■ Step 3 ı Jump 3 p. 88

1. S-The room, V-smelled, C-terrible, 2

2. S-She, V-showed, O-him, O-her pictures, 4

3. S-Harry, V-bought, O-an expensive computer, 3

4. S-He, V-found, O-the test, C-difficult, 5

5. S-We, V-saw, O-the movie, 3

6. S-My backpack, V-is, 1

7. S-The bank, V-opens, 1

8. S-The boy, V-finished, O-his homework, 3

9. S-She, V-lends, O-me, O-some money, 4

10. S-They, V-found, O-their dog, C-dead, 5

11. S-He, V-looks, C-thirsty and hungry, 2

12. S-The girl, V-speaks, O-English, 3

■ **Step 3** | Jump 4   p. 89

1. S-Bill, V-teaches, O-his students, O-math, 4

2. S-Mary, V-likes, O-a big teddy bear, 3

3. S-They, V-stayed, 1

4. S-Linda, V-plays, O-the guitar, 3

5. S-This scarf, V-feels, C-soft, 2

6. S-People, V-call, O-the kid, C-a genius, 5

7. S-The summer, V-vacation begins, 1

8. S-He, V-became, C-a wise lawyer, 2

9. S-The reporter, V-asked, O-the actor,
    O-questions, 4

10. S-The children, V-are swimming, 1

11. S-His kindness, V-made, O-her, C-happy, 5

12. S-We, V-brushed, O-our teeth, 3

■ **Step 4** | 실전 평가   p. 90

1. 주격 보어 2. 직접목적어 3. 목적격 보어 4. 목적어
5. ③ 6. ① 7. ④ 8. ② 9. ③ 10. ③ 11. bad
12. serious 13. good 14. 3형식 15. 4형식
16. dead 17. me 18. to come 19. to exericise
20. easy

1. 주격 보어는 명사 또는 형용사가 보어로 쓰여 주어를
   보충 설명해 준다.

2. 〈주어＋동사＋간접목적어(～에게)＋직접목적어(～을/
   를)〉로 이루어진 4형식 문장에서 간접목적어에는 사람
   이, 직접목적어에는 사물이 온다.

3. 목적격 보어 자리에는 명사 또는 형용사가 와서 목적
   어를 보충 설명해 준다.

6. ①번에서 wise는 목적격 보어가 아닌 주어의 성격과

상태를 나타내는 주격 보어이다.

7. 감각을 나타내는 동사(look, sound, smell, taste,
   fell)는 보어가 부사처럼 해석될 때도 있지만 형용사가
   오며, 〈주어＋동사＋보어〉로 이루어진 2형식 문장이다.

8. Joe lives in the small town.에서 in the small
   town은 수식어구로 Joe lives.로 이루어진 1형식 문장
   이다.

10. '나의 어머니는 나에게 이야기를 해 주실 것이다'라는
    뜻으로 빈칸에는 간접목적어, 직접목적어가 차례로 와야
    한다.

11. 감각동사 뒤에 보어는 부사처럼 해석되지만 형용사가
    온다.

12. 감각을 나타내는 동사에는 look, sound, smell,
    taste, feel 등이 있다.

16. 목적격 보어가 형용사인 경우에 목적어의 성질이나
    상태를 나타낸다.

■ **Step 5** | 서술형 평가   p. 92

A 1. Jenny gave Tom the gift.

  2. We named the baby Dan.

  3. Sam is standing behind the tree.

B 1. 1형식 2. 4형식 3. 2형식 4. 3형식 5. 5형식

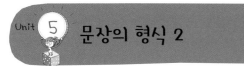

Unit 5 문장의 형식 2

Pop Quiz

1. ❶ sweet ❷ happy
2. ❶ for ❷ to
3. ❶ sad ❷ to visit

■ **Step 1** | **Check Up 1**   p. 97

1. terrible 2. sour 3. beautiful 4. smooth
5. sweet 6. comfortable 7. like 8. bitter 9. bad
10. wise, clever 11. rough 12. strong 13. strange
14. good 15. serious 16. difficult

■ **Step 1** | **Check Up 2**   p. 98

1. us math 2. for 3. to 4. of 5. her our pictures
6. to 7. him his address 8. her fairy tales 9. to
10. for 11. him candies 12. to 13. me a postcard
14. to 15. us some cookies 16. my son a desk

■ **Step 1** | **Check Up 3**   p. 99

1. for 2. to 3. to 4. to 5. to 6. for 7. me
8. to her father 9. to them 10. for her 11. me
12. for her friend 13. Susan 14. for his son
15. of him 16. his brother

■ **Step 1** | **Check Up 4**   p. 100

1. to go 2. him 3. smart 4. to take
5. to exercise 6. Butterfly 7. happy 8. difficult
9. to read 10. to join 11. to spend 12. a star
13. me 14. Prince 15. to play 16. to call

■ **Step 1** | **Check Up 5**   p. 101

1. smells delicious 2. looked, angry

---

3. tastes sweet 4. sounds beautiful 5. look, short
6. feels soft 7. tastes bitter 8. smells good
9. looks handsome

■ **Step 1** | **Check Up 6**   p. 102

1. to take 2. delicious 3. to come 4. cold
5. to cheer 6. of her 7. strange 8. for me
9. to go 10. cute 11. to his teacher 12. to them
13. to marry 14. to help 15. to John
16. to exercise

■ **Step 2** | **Build Up 1**   p. 103

1. looks short 2. sounded good 3. feels, smooth
4. tastes sour 5. smells sweet 6. to 7. of 8. for
9. to 10. for 11. to 12. to

■ **Step 2** | **Build Up 2**   p. 104

1. David gave a birthday present to him.
2. We made a big chocolate cake for Lisa.
3. Daniel bought a yellow scarf for his mom.
4. My sister asked a strange question of me.
5. Peter buys an interesting book for his cousin.
6. Mr. Johnson taught history to them.
7. My aunt cooked spaghetti for her daughter.
8. Tony wrote an e-mail to his friend.
9. He always asks difficult questions of us.
10. The artist showed some pictures to her.

■ **Step 2** | **Build Up 3**   p. 105

1. His father bought a pink dress for her.
2. Tom made the children nice kites.
3. Andy gave a lot of roses to me.
4. My grandfather told many stories to us.
5. The girl asked me some questions.
6. The man gave her a diamond ring.
7. My uncle sent a Christmas present to me.
8. The teacher bought them some snacks.

9. The secretary handed him the book.

10. Dave lent his bicycle to my brother.

■ **Step 3 ∣ Jump 1** p. 106

1. sound, smell, taste, 형용사 **2.** like **3.** 수여동사
4. 간접목적어, 3, English to the students, to, for, ask
5. 명사, 형용사, to부정사

■ **Step 3 ∣ Jump 2** p. 107

1. of me **2.** to exercise **3.** sweet **4.** to us
5. sad **6.** to go **7.** to us **8.** busy **9.** the box
10. to take **11.** good **12.** for me **13.** to complete
14. basketball **15.** like **16.** his sons

■ **Step 3 ∣ Jump 3** p. 108

1. to come to the party
2. writes her a long letter
3. tastes bitter
4. showed his album to us
5. made her sad
6. sounds strange
7. made a snowman for me
8. pass me the sugar
9. look happy today
10. asked her name of me
11. called the baby Cathy

■ **Step 3 ∣ Jump 4** p. 109

1. Sally and Ann look beautiful.
2. The chicken soup smells delicious.
3. The silk feels smooth and soft.
4. His voice sounds tired.
5. Chocolate tastes sweet and bitter.
6. My brother made me angry.
7. The foreigner asked us some questions.
8. Mark made a model car for him.
9. My mother found the box empty.
10. I wanted him to learn English.

■ **Step 4 ∣ 실전 평가** p. 110

1. ① **2.** ② **3.** ④ **4.** ③ **5.** ④ **6.** ① **7.** ② **8.** ④
9. ③ **10.** ④ **11.** ② **12.** ④ **13.** ② **14.** ④ **15.** ②
16. ② **17.** to **18.** funny **19.** It sounds strange.
20. The cloth feels smooth.

1. 4형식을 3형식으로 전환할 때 전치사가 필요한데, 전치사 for가 사용된 것으로 보아 made가 와야 한다.

2. 4형식을 3형식으로 전환한 문장으로 동사가 ask인 것으로 보아 전치사 of가 와야 한다.

3. 감각을 나타내내는 동사 look, sound, smell, taste, feel 등 뒤에 보어는 부사처럼 해석되지만 형용사가 온다. 따라서 ④번 sounds great가 되어야 한다.

4. taste 다음에는 반드시 형용사가 온다.

5. 5형식 문장의 목적격 보어에는 명사, 형용사, to부정사 등이 올 수 있다.

6. ①번은 4형식 문장으로 직접 목적어이고 나머지는 5형식 문장으로 목적격 보어이다.

7. 4형식을 3형식으로 전환할 때 전치사가 필요한데, for를 쓰는 동사는 make, buy, cook, sing, get 등이다.

9. 4형식 문장에서 간접 목적어＋직접 목적어로 쓰인 경우에는 전치사가 필요 없다.

10. 5형식 문장에서 동사 advise의 목적격 보어로 동사가 오는 경우에는 to부정사의 형태로 쓴다.

11. 4형식을 3형식으로 전환할 때 전치사가 필요한데, to를 쓰는 동사는 give, send, bring, teach, show, tell, write, pass, lend 등이다. ②번은 동사에 made가 있으므로 전치사 for를 써야 한다.

12. ①～③번은 4형식 문장에 '～에게 ～을 (해)주다'라는 뜻이 포함되어 있는 수여동사이다.

13. ②번은 〈주어＋동사＋간접 목적어＋직접 목적어〉로 이루어진 4형식 문장이고 나머지는 〈주어＋동사＋목적어＋목적격 보어〉로 이루어진 5형식 문장이다.

14. smell 다음에는 부사 greatly가 아닌 형용사 great가 와야 한다.

16. ②번에서 간접 목적어 us를 뒤로 이동하여 3형식 문장으로 만들 경우 간접 목적어 앞에 전치사를 넣어야 하

는데 동사 teach이므로 to us가 되어야 한다.

■ **Step 5** | 서술형 평가   p. 112

A **1.** sounds beautiful **2.** feels dirty
B **1.** a nice hat to **2.** a teddy bear for
C **1.** to eat more vegetable for his health
  2. wants him to help her with her homework
  3. wants him to spend more time with him

Unit 6 현재완료

Pop Quiz

I. ❶ lost ❷ gone

■ **Step 1** | Check Up 1   p. 117

1. cut **2.** met **3.** won **4.** gotten **5.** sent **6.** taken
7. brought **8.** written **9.** kept **10.** told **11.** taught
12. slept **13.** quit **14.** sat **15.** built **16.** known
17. made **18.** become **19.** lost **20.** stolen
21. seen **22.** been **23.** gone **24.** stood

■ **Step 1** | Check Up 2   p. 118

1. read, read **2.** slept, slept **3.** said, said
4. sold, sold **5.** put, put **6.** threw, thrown

7. left, left **8.** gave, given **9.** rose, risen
10. drove, driven **11.** caught, caught
12. fell, fallen **13.** swam, swum **14.** ran, run
15. lived, lived **16.** found, found **17.** drank, drunk
18. fought, fought

■ **Step 1** | Check Up 3   p. 119

1. seen **2.** lost **3.** gone **4.** lived **5.** finished
6. completed **7.** stolen **8.** left **9.** arrived
10. broken **11.** driven **12.** painted **13.** been
14. visited **15.** slept **16.** sung

■ **Step 1** | Check Up 4   p. 120

1. have, eaten **2.** has, been **3.** have, ridden
4. has, solved **5.** has, worked **6.** have, been
7. has, gone **8.** Have, seen **9.** has, spent
10. Has, met **11.** has, lost **12.** have, arrived
13. has, come **14.** has, been **15.** Have, taken
16. have, left

■ **Step 1** | Check Up 5   p. 121

1. The girl hasn't learned to tie the shoes.
2. I haven't lost the textbook.
3. Tom and Dan haven't seen a ghost.
4. Sarah hasn't finished her work.
5. We haven't forgotten his name.
6. They haven't cleaned the classroom.
7. My parents haven't lived in New York.
8. The boy hasn't broken the window.
9. I haven't worked at the museum.
10. They haven't done the homework.

■ **Step 1** | Check Up 6   p. 122

1. Has she bought a new dress?
2. Has Jonathan gone to France?
3. Have they read the book before?
4. Has Jenny been in Japan for five years?

5. Have you lost my toy airplane?

6. Has Amy lived in many places?

7. Has he traveled around the world?

8. Has Jason found his new job?

9. Have they already finished the project?

10. Have you seen a double rainbow before?

■ Step 2 ı Build Up 1   p. 123

1. has been 2. arrived 3. taught 4. have seen
5. has lived 6. have known 7. had 8. rang
9. has been 10. lost 11. bought 12. has played
13. visited 14. played 15. have heard 16. sold

■ Step 2 ı Build Up 2   p. 124

1. has, learned, since 2. has, just, finished
3. Have, ever, seen 4. have, never, read
5. have, known, for 6. have, been, once
7. have, met 8. has, not, seen
9. has, already, borrowed 10. has, swum, for

■ Step 2 ı Build Up 3   p. 125

1. have, ever, played 2. have, lived, for
3. has, never, won 4. Have, heard, before
5. has, gone, to 6. have, been, for
7. has, already, cleaned 8. has, been, since
9. has, not, understood 10. has, taught, for

■ Step 3 ı Jump 1   p. 126

1. 현재완료

2. 계속, have, been, 완료, has, just, finished, 결과,
   has, gone, 경험, Have, ever, been

3. 현재완료, 과거

4. 과거, yesterday, last year, ago

■ Step 3 ı Jump 2   p. 127

1. went 2. been 3. paid 4. have lost 5. finished

6. moved 7. for 8. lost 9. seen 10. since
11. have not 12. been 13. has been 14. broken
15. climbed 16. learned

■ Step 3 ı Jump 3   p. 128

1. Somebody has stolen my bike. – 결과

2. I have waited for her for one hour. – 계속

3. They have been to Japan once. – 경험

4. He has just finished his homework. – 완료

5. Have you ever played golf? – 경험

6. We have not written the letter yet. – 완료

■ Step 3 ı Jump 4   p. 129

1. I have lost my hat 2. He has lived in Seoul for

3. has gone to New York

4. has lived in Tokyo since 2011

5. has broken his leg 6. has left for China

7. has dated Ashley since

8. has had a new car since

■ Step 4 ı 실전 평가   p. 130

1. ④ 2. ③ 3. ① 4. ② 5. ② 6. ④ 7. been
8. has lived 9. has left 10. ① 11. ④ 12. ②
13. ③ 14. ① 15. ④ 16. ②
17. He has not[hasn't] seen her since last Friday.
18. Have his brothers bought him a present?
19. have learned 20. has lost

1. 과거에 일어난 일이 현재까지 영향을 미칠 때 현재완료
   시제를 쓰는데 현재완료는 have+과거분사이다.

2. 현재완료 문장의 부정문은 have나 has 다음에 not을
   붙여서 나타낸다. 또한 have not은 haven't로, has
   not은 hasn't로 줄여서 쓸 수 있다.

3. just now, yesterday, last weekend 등 명백한
   과거를 나타내는 말들은 과거시제에만 사용한다.

4. 대화의 A는 Have가 있는 것으로 보아 현재완료 의문
   문으로 과거분사인 seen이 와야 하며, B는 과거를 나

타내는 ago가 있는 것으로 보아 과거시제인 saw가 와야 한다.

5. 현재완료 문장에서 주어가 3인칭 단수형일 때는 have 가 아닌 has를 쓴다.

6. 현재완료로 물어볼 경우에는 현재완료로 답을 해야 하는데, ④번은 명백한 과거를 나타내는 부사 ago가 있는 것으로 봐서 올 수 없다.

7. '어디에 있다'라는 뜻으로 be동사가 들어가야 하는데, 현재완료 문장이므로 be의 과거분사인 been이 들어가야 한다.

10. '평생을 서울에서 살아오고 있다'는 뜻으로 과거부터 현재까지 이어진 일을 나타내고 있으므로 am lived 는 have lived가 되어야 한다.

11. 보기는 과거부터 현재까지 하고 있는 일을 나타내고 있으므로 현재완료의 계속으로 쓰였다. ①번은 경험을 나타내고, ②번은 결과, ③번은 완료를 나타낸다.

12. 현재완료가 과거부터 현재까지 해 본 일을 나타낼 때에는 경험을 나타내며, 경험을 나타내는 경우는 보통 before, once, ever, never 등과 사용된다.

13. 한국전쟁이 1950년에 일어난 것은 명백한 과거를 나타내므로 과거시제로 나타내야 한다.

15. ①번은 주어가 3인칭 단수형인 He로 has가 되어야 하며, ②번은 과거분사인 eaten으로, ③번은 과거를 나타내는 부사구가 있으므로 과거시제로 나타내야 한다.

■ **Step 5 | 서술형 평가** p. 132

A 1. have just eaten
2. have just gone
3. has just arrived

B 1. has sent an e-mail
2. hasn't[has not] walked his
3. has cleaned his room with his brother
4. hasn't[has not] written a diary

Unit 7 수동태

Pop Quiz

1. ❶ is fixed ❷ is loved
2. ❶ was written ❷ be visited

■ **Step 1 | Check Up 1** p. 141

1. made 2. hurt 3. built 4. read 5. invented
6. said 7. taught 8. seen 9. cut 10. taken
11. sent 12. stolen 13. known 14. eaten
15. written 16. painted 17. bought 18. given
19. kept 20. broken 21. spoken 22. shown
23. ridden 24. thrown

■ **Step 1 | Check Up 2** p. 142

1. was written 2. built 3. are carried 4. be
5. are seen 6. finish 7. bought 8. was broken
9. given 10. was invented 11. read 12. made
13. is cleaned 14. are eaten 15. ordered
16. was killed

■ **Step 1 | Check Up 3** p. 143

1. was built 2. wrote 3. was discovered
4. was born 5. were made 6. are worn 7. painted
8. were taught 9. be seen 10. was broken
11. deliver 12. wrote 13. were taken
14. is spoken 15. was visited 16. found

■ **Step 1 | Check Up 4** p. 144

1. will be repaired by 2. were used by
3. is loved by 4. were destroyed by
5. will be driven by 6. can be paid by
7. was played by 8. were made by
9. was thrown, by 10. was posted by

1. were loved by everyone
2. are cleaned every day by Jill
3. was respected by the students
4. were made for her sons by her
5. was parked in the street by John
6. is read each year by many people
7. is learned all over the world by people
8. were given some apple juice by her
9. was bought for me by my father
10. is used every day by many people

1. were told a funny story by Brian, was told to them by Brian
2. was sent a long message by Susan, was sent to Mark by Susan
3. is asked a question by the students, is asked of him by the students
4. was given a diamond ring by Thomas, was given to her by Thomas
5. are taught science by Mr. Brown, are taught to them by Mr. Brown
6. was sent a health checklist by the doctor, was sent to her by the doctor
7. was made for me by my brother
8. was bought for her by Billy

1. The postcard was sent last Monday by Amy.
2. The red roses are loved by Cathy.
3. The children were invited by them.
4. The bathroom was cleaned by my mom.
5. The picture was drawn yesterday by her.
6. The fence will be painted by Jonathan.
7. The play was written by Shakespeare.
8. The thick book can be read by the little boy.
9. The ladder was carried by Dan and Tom.
10. The Statue of Liberty was made by a Frenchman.

1. This scary movie was made by the director.
2. Some cookies and candies were eaten by the kids.
3. Your sister will be helped by your father.
4. The moon is seen at night by people.
5. The book can be copied by the secretary.
6. The brick house was built by the farmer.
7. The wild animals were protected by them.
8. The windows were broken by the children.
9. The light bulb was invented by Thomas Edison.
10. Alice and Lucy are loved by everyone.

1. The hunters catch the bears.
2. The man washed the cars.
3. Many people use credit cards.
4. A thief stole Ashley's purse.
5. The mayor visited the park.
6. Dad made us some sandwiches.
7. Ann and Joe made these bags.
8. They love soccer matches.
9. She bought me a CD player.
10. We canceled the meeting.

1. 능동태, 수동태   2. (1) 목적어   (2) 과거분사   (3) 목적격, The letter was written by me.
3. 1, 2   4. be, will, be   5. be, 과거분사
6. 직접목적어, 직접목적어   7. by, 행위자

1. loved   2. be   3. wrote   4. by   5. her   6. stole
7. invented   8. were   9. revealed   10. to Jane

11. be solved 12. saved 13. were 14. grows
15. caught 16. created

■ **Step 3 | Jump 3**   p. 152

1. Spanish is spoken in Mexico by people.
2. David was elected our class leader.
3. He will be given a special prize by us.
4. A computer was bought for me by my mother.
5. My brother found the key on the bed.
6. The music was composed last month by her.
7. The camera was given to him by us.
8. Coffee is grown in hot countries by people.
9. She sent the letter to the wrong address.
10. Korean food will be ordered by them.

■ **Step 3 | Jump 4**   p. 153

1. Chocolate is loved by the children.
2. The elevator will be repaired by him.
3. The package was delivered by the mailman.
4. Fresh vegetables were served by them.
5. The wild animals were caught by the hunter.
6. We were invited to the party by Ann.
7. America was discovered by Columbus.
8. A thief was arrested yesterday by the woman.
9. The cities will be connected by the train.
10. The robber is chased by the young men.

■ **Step 4 | 실전 평가**   p. 154

1. ③ 2. ④ 3. was written 4. was broken 5. ②
6. ① 7. ② 8. ③ 9. ④ 10. ① 11. is read
12. are helped
13. was invented by Thomas Edison, invented the light bulb
14. was written by Leo Tolstoy, wrote the book *War and Peace*

1. 수동태는 무슨 일이 일어났는지에 중점을 둔 문장으로

대상이 주어가 되며 형태는 〈be동사+과거분사〉이다.
2. 수동태의 현재와 과거시제는 be동사로 나타내고, 미래 시제는 〈will+be+과거분사〉로 나타낸다.
3. 능동태 문장을 수동태 문장을 바꿀 때, 1. 능동태의 목적어를 주어로 한다. 2. 동사를 'be동사+과거분사'의 형태로 고친다. 이때, 새로운 주어에 맞게 be동사를 사용한다. 3. 능동태의 주어를 'by+목적어'의 형태로 고친다.
5. 간접목적어와 직접목적어를 갖는 동사인 give, ask, tell, teach, show 등은 두 가지의 수동태를 만들 수 있는데, 직접목적어를 주어로 하는 경우, 간접목적어 앞에 전치사(to, for, of)를 써 준다.
7. 수동태 문장에서 by+행위자를 생략할 수가 있는데, 행위자가 일반적인 사람일 때이거나 행위자를 모르거나 중요하지 않을 때 생략할 수 있다.
9. 가르침을 받는 것이기 때문에 teaching이 taught가 되어야 한다.
10. ②~④번은 인형을 받은 사람이 Julia이고 ①번은 인형을 준 사람이 Julia이다.
11. 수동태 만드는 법에 따라 1. 능동태의 목적어를 주어로 한다. 2. 동사를 'be동사+과거분사'의 형태로 고친다. 이때, 새로운 주어에 맞게 be동사를 사용한다. 3. 능동태의 주어를 'by+목적어'의 형태로 고친다.
13. 능동태는 〈invented+목적어〉를 쓰고 수동태는 〈목적어+was invented by〉로 쓴다.
14. 능동태는 〈wrote+목적어〉를 쓰고 수동태는 〈목적어+was written by〉로 쓴다.

■ **Step 5 | 서술형 평가**   p. 156

A 1. are worn by kangaroo
  2. was seen by some boys
B 1. were invented by the Wright Brothers
  2. was written by O. Henry

Unit 8 관계대명사

■ **Step 1** | **Check Up 1** p. 161

1. 선행사 –that girl, 관계대명사–who
2. 선행사–a friend, 관계대명사–whose
3. 선행사–the boy, 관계대명사–who
4. 선행사–the only foreigner, 관계대명사–that
5. 선행사–the pen, 관계대명사–which
6. 선행사–The park, 관계대명사–which
7. 선행사–a big house, 관계대명사–whose
8. 선행사–the girl, 관계대명사–whom
9. 선행사–the girl and her dog, 관계대명사–that
10. 선행사–The woman, 관계대명사–who
11. 선행사–The necklace, 관계대명사–which
12. 선행사–all the money, 관계대명사–that
13. 선행사–the bike, 관계대명사–that
14. 선행사–a child, 관계대명사–whose
15. 선행사–The lake, 관계대명사–which
16. 선행사–a car, 관계대명사–whose

■ **Step 1** | **Check Up 2** p. 162

1. who 2. that 3. that 4. which 5. which
6. which 7. that 8. whose 9. who 10. which
11. that 12. which 13. who 14. whose 15. which
16. whom

■ **Step 1** | **Check Up 3** p. 163

1. 주어–The man, 동사–likes
2. 주어–The actor, 동사–was 3. 주어–We, 동사–met
4. 주어–They, 동사–saw 5. 주어–We, 동사–know

6. 주어–They, 동사–have 7. 주어–Julia, 동사–wore
8. 주어–The man, 동사–is
9. 주어–The bag, 동사–was
10. 주어–They, 동사–were 11. 주어–John, 동사–lost
12. 주어–I, 동사–like 13. 주어–The man, 동사–is
14. 주어–you, 동사–have
15. 주어–The people, 동사–were
16. 주어–I, 동사–know

■ **Step 1** | **Check Up 4** p. 164

1. which are 2. which 3. which 4. who is
5. which is 6. who is 7. who were 8. whom
9. which was 10. which 11. who 12. who
13. which 14. which are 15. which 16. which is

■ **Step 1** | **Check Up 5** p. 165

1. is 2. are 3. are 4. lives 5. is 6. was 7. help
8. are 9. are 10. has 11. are 12. is 13. is
14. plays 15. is 16. work

■ **Step 1** | **Check Up 6** p. 166

1. whom 2. which 3. who 4. that 5. whom
6. who 7. whose 8. which 9. that 10. who
11. whose 12. that 13. which 14. whose
15. that 16. whose

■ **Step 2** | **Build Up 1** p. 167

1. They ate the food which[that] was cooked by her.
2. The man is Billy who(m)[that] we saw in the theater.
3. I still have the teddy bear which[that] you gave me.
4. There is a boy whose name is Peter.
5. Tom is wearing blue jeans which[that] are new.
6. Do you know the girl who[that] Tom is walking

with?

7. The scarf which[that] Lisa is wearing is very expensive.

8. She is a teacher who(m)[that] I met yesterday.

9. Look at the girl and her dog that are running.

10. I like the computer which[that] Brian is using now.

■ Step 2 | Build Up 2   p. 168

1. I live in a new house whose roof is brown.

2. I know the children whose father is a police officer.

3. The people are very kind who[that] she met last night.

4. I like Picasso whose paintings are unique.

5. We packed the things which[that] we needed for camping.

6. I know the girl who[that] can speak three languages.

7. This is a woman who[that] came from Canada.

8. Ann was carrying a bag which[that] was very light.

9. I see a little boy who[that] is riding a donkey.

10. Look at the lion which[that] is running after the deer.

■ Step 2 | Build Up 3   p. 169

1. The house which[that] is in the picture was built in 2000.

2. The frog which[that] jumps two meters high is his.

3. He married a woman who[that] was from French.

4. This is a storybook which[that] is good for children.

5. I met a girl whose mother is a famous pianist.

6. This is the mountain which[that] I took nice pictures.

7. This is the best book that I have ever read.

8. The watch which[that] I bought made in the US.

9. The apples which[that] grow in my orchard are sweet.

10. I gave her all the money that I have.

■ Step 3 | Jump 1   p. 170

1. 접속사, 대명사 2. 명사, 선행사

3. 목적격, who, which, that, who, whose, which, which, that, that 4. whose 5. 동사, 주어

6. that, 사람, that 7. be동사, 목적격

■ Step 3 | Jump 2   p. 171

1. whose 2. which[that] 3. who[that] 4. lives

5. that 6. which[that] 7. are 8. whose

9. who[that] 10. that 11. which[that] 12. that

13. whose 14. whose 15. who(m) 16. that

■ Step 3 | Jump 3   p. 172

1. Look at the boys who[that] are singing on the stage. / Look at the boys singing on the stage.

2. The toys which[that] are in the box are made in Japan. / The toys in the box are made in Japan.

3. He is the kind man who[that] she gave the key. / He is the kind man she gave the key.

4. This is the picture which[that] was painted by my sister. / This is the picture painted by my sister.

5. The coffee which[that] I bought from London smells good. / The coffee I bought from London smells good.

6. He can borrow the books which[that] are in my room. / He can borrow the books in my room.

7. He who[that] is talking with them is my son. / He talking with them is my son.

1. is the subject that I like most
2. the boy and his dog that are running
3. a cat that has sharp teeth
4. a student who can answer the question
5. looking for a boy whose name is Peter
6. the same bag that I lost yesterday
7. house whose roof has small windows
8. which we bought is on the hill

1. ④ 2. ② 3. looks → look 4. whose → which
5. ③ 6. which we cooked 7. ① 8. ④ 9. ①
10. ④ 11. who 12. which
13. Do you kow the woman who took care of animals?
14. He is an actor who stars in a lot of movies.

1. 관계대명사는 대명사처럼 주격, 소유격, 목적격이 있다. 선행사가 사람일 때는 관계대명사 who가, 동물이나 사물일 때는 which가, 사람이나 동물, 사물일 때는 that이 온다.
2. 그 늙은 사람의 머리카락을 나타내므로 who의 소유격인 whose가 와야 한다.
3. 주어가 people로 복수이므로 동사의 경우 동사원형이 와야 한다.
4. 책을 빌린 것을 나타내므로 목적격인 which가 와야 한다.
5. 관계대명사 that은 who(m)나 which 대신 쓰인다.
7. 보기의 that은 관계대명사 that이다. ②번은 지시형용사 that이고 ③번은 접속사 that이다. 또한 ④번은 지시대명사 that이다.
10. ④번에는 소유격이 들어가야 하는데 that은 소유격으로는 사용하지 않는다.

A 1. ③, who[that] 2. ②, which[that]
   3. ①, who[that]
B 1. The boy is my friend. He can speak Chinese.
   2. An elephant is an animal. It has a very big nose.

1. ③ 2. ④ 3. ① 4. ② 5. ③ 6. ② 7. ④ 8. ①
9. ② 10. ③ 11. ① 12. ② 13. ④ 14. ① 15. ④
16. ③ 17. never 18. ③
19. is respected by the students
20. I know the man who[that] is an actor.

1. to부정사는 'to+동사원형'의 형태로, 명사나 형용사, 또는 부사로 쓰이는데, 동사의 의미는 가지고 있지만, 문장의 동사로 쓰이지 않는다. to부정사가 명사 뒤에 와서 형용사 역할을 하며 명사를 수식하는 경우에는 '~할'로 해석한다.
2. like는 목적어로 to부정사와 동명사를 취하는 동사이다.
3. 전치사 뒤에는 명사가 오는데, 동사가 올 경우에는 동명사의 형태로 쓴다.
4. decide는 목적어로 to부정사를 취하는 동사이다.
5. to부정사의 명사적 쓰임은 to부정사가 문장에서 명사 역할인 주어, 목적어, 보어로 경우이다. ①번은 형용사적 쓰임이고 ②, ④번은 부사적 쓰임이다.
6. to부정사가 앞에 있는 명사 water를 꾸며주는 역할을 하고 있다. 따라서 보기처럼 형용사적 쓰임으로 것은 ②번이다.
7. -e로 끝나는 동사는 e를 삭제하고 -ing를 붙인다. 따라서 dance의 현재분사는 dancing이다.
8. remember는 동명사와 to부정사 모두 쓰지만 의미가 달라지는 동사로, remember -ing는 '~했던 것을 기억하다'이고 remember to부정사는 '~해야 하는 것을 기억하다'라는 뜻이다.
9. 보기에서 동명사 selling은 문장에서 보어 역할을 하고

있으며 보어로 사용된 동명사를 찾으면 된다.

10. 4형식을 3형식으로 전환할 때 전치사가 필요한데, make, buy, cook, sing, get 등의 동사는 전치사 for를 필요로 한다.

11. 간접 목적어 me가 뒤로 이동하면서 4형식 문장을 3형식 문장으로 바꾼 문장이다. 그런데 전치사 of가 있으므로 전치사 of를 필요로 하는 동사는 ask가 있는 문장을 찾으면 된다.

12. 감각을 나타내내는 동사에는 look, sound, smell, taste, feel 등이 있는데, 감각동사 뒤에 보어는 부사처럼 해석되지만 형용사가 온다.

14. 현재완료의 완료로 빈칸에는 just나 already가 들어갈 수 있다.

15. 현재완료의 계속으로 숫자가 나온 것으로 보아 for가 들어가야 한다.

16. 보기는 '누군가 나의 자전거를 가져가서 지금은 없다.'라는 뜻으로 현재완료의 결과이다. ①, ②번은 경험, ④번은 계속의 의미이다.

18. 수동태는 be동사+과거분사의 형태로 주어가 누군가에 의해 어떤 행동을 당하는 문장이다.

20. 관계대명사는 두 문장을 하나로 이어주는 접속사 역할과 명사를 대신하는 대명사의 역할을 동시에 하는데, 관계대명사 앞에 있는 선행사가 사람인 경우에는 who를 이용하여 나타낸다.

■ Final Test 2   p. 180

1. ① 2. ③ 3. ② 4. looks 5. ④ 6. ④ 7. ② 8. ①
9. ② 10. ③ 11. ③ 12. ④ 13. ① 14. ④ 15. ③
16. ④ 17. ③ 18. ① 19. The bears are caught by the hunters. 20. ③

1. 문장에 to go가 있는 것으로 보아 to부정사를 목적어로 취하는 동사가 빈칸에 들어가야 한다. enjoy는 목적어로 동명사를 취하는 동사이다.

2. 문장의 빈칸에는 목적어인 명사가 와야 한다. 의문사+to부정사는 문장에서 명사처럼 사용되며 '~해야 할지'로 해석한다.

3. 목적어에 동명사가 온 것으로 보아 빈칸에는 동명사를 목적어로 취하는 동사가 와야 한다.

5. ④번에서 to eat는 앞에 있는 명사 food를 수식하며 형용사 역할을 한다.

6. ①번은 명사적 쓰임이고, ②번과 ③번은 형용사적 쓰임으로 쓰였다.

7. 보기는 동명사로 형태는 동사 뒤에 -ing를 붙이는데, 현재분사와 형태는 같지만 문장에서의 역할은 다르다. 현재분사는 be동사와 함께 쓰여 진행형을 만들거나 명사 앞이나 뒤에서 형용사처럼 명사를 수식한다.

8. 4형식 문장을 3형식 문장으로 바꿀 때, 즉 간접 목적어를 뒤로 뺄 경우에는 전치사가 필요한데 sent는 전치사 to를 필요로 한다.

9. 4형식 문장을 3형식 문장으로 바꿀 때, ask는 전치사 of를 필요로 한다.

10. 4형식 문장을 3형식 문장으로 바꿀 때, make는 전치사 for를 필요로 한다.

11. 동명사가 주어로 쓰인 문장은 to부정사로 바꾸어 가주어 it을 사용하여 나타낼 수 있다.

14. sleep의 과거분사는 slept이다.

15. 과거의 일이 현재까지 영향을 미칠 때 현재완료 문장을 사용하는데, 형태는 have+과거분사로 쓴다.

16. ①~③번은 과거에 시작된 일이 지금도 계속되고 있는 계속의 쓰임이고 ④번은 시작된 일이 막 끝난 것을 나타낸 완료의 쓰임이다.

17. ③번은 완료의 쓰임이고 나머지는 과거의 경험을 나타낸 경험의 쓰임이다.

20. 두 문장을 하나로 연결할 때 관계대명사 앞에 있는 선행사가 사물인 경우에는 which를 이용하여 나타낸다.